David Smith is Lecturer in Urban Mi tianity at the International Christian was previously Principal of Northumbria Bible College and Co-Director of the Whitefield Institute in Oxford. He has taught at various seminaries in Africa and Asia, and was for a number of years a lecturer at the Samuel Bill Theological College in Nigeria. He has previously published *Transforming the World? The Social Impact of British Evangelicalism* (1998), *Crying in the Wilderness* (2000), *Mission After Christendom* (2003) and *Against the Stream: Christianity and Mission in an Age of Globalization* (2003).

Christ at Emmaus by Rembrandt (1606–1669)
© Photo SCALA, Florence, Musée Jacquemart-André/Inst. de France, Paris, 1999.

MOVING TOWARDS EMMAUS

EMMAUS

Hope in a time of uncertainty

David Smith

First published in Great Britain in 2007

Society for Promoting Christian Knowledge
36 Causton Street
London SW1P 4ST

British Library Cataloguing-in-Publication Data
A catalogue record for this book is available from the British Library

ISBN 978–0–281–05909–6

1 3 5 7 9 10 8 6 4 2

Typeset by Graphicraft Limited, Hong Kong
Printed in Great Britain by Ashford Colour Press

Produced on paper from sustainable forests

Contents

———•·●·•———

Preface

The Old Testament scholar Walter Brueggemann published a book a few years ago with the intriguing title *Texts that Linger, Words that Explode*. He suggested that the prophetic writings of ancient Israel, originally spoken with great power by people inspired with alternative visions of the future of the world, became *lingering* texts, preserved, revered and read by generations of faithful people. They came to be recognized as sacred Scripture and the story they contained shaped the identity and kept alive the hopes of those who worshipped the God to whom the prophets bore witness. This work of preserving the texts Brueggemann attributes to scribal activity because, as he puts it, 'When "prophecy ends" scribes guard the text that results from prophetic utterance' (Brueggemann, 2000, 18).

However, Brueggemann suggests that from time to time these ancient texts suddenly burst into new life; *exploding* with unexpected relevance and power in new situations. They became again, in new and surprising ways, *prophetic* as the old words resonated in historical and cultural contexts different from those in which they were originally uttered. Brueggemann discusses a number of examples of prophetic texts that can be seen bursting into fresh life *within* the Bible itself, and the study of the history of biblical interpretation across the centuries would suggest many examples of the kind of process he has described.

This present book is a modest attempt to suggest the ways in which a familiar New Testament narrative may be recognized as an 'exploding text' at the present time. The beautiful Lukan story of the 'walk to Emmaus' has been loved and revered across the centuries and there is considerable evidence of its continuing power in a wide variety of cultural contexts.

However, my proposal in this book is that this narrative can be read as having particular relevance in a historical and cultural situation that is described as both post-Christian and post-modern. It is my belief that in this precise situation, the Emmaus story resonates with fresh, previously unrecognized meaning. I have reached this conclusion partly as the result of the way in which this story has spoken to me at a deeply personal level, but also because of the response I have found when this narrative has been used in the way outlined in this book as the basis for teaching and discussion in various settings over the past few years.

I must confess at this point that there is a real element of risk in the task I have undertaken here in that I have consciously moved beyond the kind of formal exegesis of the biblical text that is usually regarded as indispensable to Christian preaching and teaching. I take heart again from Brueggemann who observes that ancient texts explode into fresh life only when teachers and preachers are willing to move beyond the 'scribal' activities that may be equated with the technical, scholarly aspects of interpretation, and display 'a capacity for imagination and intuition, coupled with courage' in hearing and speaking these texts in contemporary situations. Courage is not, of course, the same thing as recklessness, and while I hope my reading of this story displays a little of the former quality, my respect for the authority of the Bible means that I would certainly not wish to be found guilty of the latter.

One more word of introduction: in what follows I have quite deliberately endeavoured to read this great story in *dialogue* with people beyond the confines of the Christian tradition. I make no apology for this at all; indeed it has increasingly seemed to me that one of the great tragedies of our time is that so much Christian speaking and writing is designed for purely internal consumption. The word 'tragedy' is appropriate here, both because such religious navel-gazing betrays the intention of Luke, the original author of this Gospel, and because it fails to recognize the opportunities for friendship, conversation and dialogue that a pluralist culture has made both possible and urgently necessary. Exactly half a century ago, at the height of the frantic debates in Western theology concerning the 'death of God', one of the sanest thinkers at that time observed that the real tragedy of the era was that 'doubt has become immune to faith, and faith has dissociated itself from doubt' (Vahanian, 1957, 13). What makes the present context so significant, it seems to me, is that social and religious apartheid of that kind, which resulted in Christians and people of other faiths, or of no faith, living segregated lives with no real contact or interaction with each other, is now breaking down. Christians, chastened by the experience of their increasing cultural marginalization, and humanists, troubled by the fading of the Enlightenment dream, are now better able to recognize the truth of Gabriel Vahanian's observation: 'Nothing is worse than a dead faith, except a dead doubt.'

That being so, it is my hope that this book will be read by people of all faiths, and of no faith, and that they will recognize it as a credible Christian contribution to the discussion that must be had concerning the future of our troubled and threatened world. I write unashamedly as an orthodox Christian and my clear intention is to bear witness to my own faith, but at the same time I wish to recognize the common ground that exists between Christians and other people in a 'time of uncertainty' when, as the following pages will suggest, we seem to be thrown together on the road to Emmaus.

I wish to thank my colleagues at International Christian College in Glasgow for their friendship and support, and for the creation of an environment in which the kind of issues being raised here are discussed on many mornings in our staff room. I am especially grateful to Jean Munro and Gwen Henderson whose comments on the early chapters at the start of this project gave me the encouragement I needed to press on. Sections of the book were read by René Padilla, Chris Wright and Pauline Hoggarth and they offered very helpful observations. Mention of Pauline Hoggarth leads me to acknowledge the considerable debt I owe to Scripture Union

International for giving me the privilege of addressing their staff training conferences in France and South Africa in the past few years. The response of leaders from around the world to an early attempt to articulate the significance of this text for today first alerted me to the dynamic power of the Emmaus story and was a significant stage in conceiving and bringing to birth the book you now hold in your hands. Finally, I must acknowledge my debt to the late Professor James Thrower of the University of Aberdeen, whose inspiring teaching expanded my understanding of the contemporary world, and whose friendship taught me the vital importance of genuine dialogue concerning the ultimate issues of life and death.

In view of the comments made above concerning the risky element in this enterprise, it is more than usually necessary to say that none of the friends mentioned bears responsibility for the final form this study has taken; the risks are mine alone, as are any errors of fact or judgement.

David Smith

The story

Now that same day two of them were going to a village called Emmaus, about seven miles from Jerusalem. They were talking with each other about everything that had happened. As they talked and discussed these things with each other, Jesus himself came up and walked along with them; but they were kept from recognising him.

He asked them, 'What are you discussing together as you walk along?' They stood still, their faces downcast. One of them, named Cleopas, asked him, 'Are you the only one living in Jerusalem who doesn't know the things that have happened there in these days?'

'What things?' he asked.

'About Jesus of Nazareth,' they replied. 'He was a prophet, powerful in word and deed before God and all the people. The chief priests and our rulers handed him over to be sentenced to death, and they crucified him; but we had hoped that he was the one who was going to restore Israel. And what is more, it is the third day since all this took place. In addition, some of our women amazed us. They went to the tomb early this morning but didn't find his body. They came and told us that they had seen a vision of angels, who said he was alive. Then some of our companions went to the tomb and found it just as the women had said, but him they did not see.'

He said to them, 'How foolish you are, and how slow of heart to believe all that the prophets have spoken! Did not the Christ have to suffer these things and then enter into his glory?' And beginning with Moses and all the Prophets, he explained to them what was said in all the Scriptures concerning himself.

As they approached the village to which they were going, Jesus acted as if he were going further. But they urged him strongly, 'Stay with us, for it is nearly evening; the day is almost over.' So he went in to stay with them.

When he was at the table with them, he took bread, gave thanks, broke it and began to give it to them. Then their eyes were opened and they recognised him, and he disappeared out of their sight. They asked each other, 'Were not our hearts burning within us while he talked with us on the road and opened the Scriptures to us?' Then they got up and returned at once to Jerusalem. There they found the eleven and those with them, assembled together and saying, 'It is true! The Lord has risen and appeared to Simon.' Then the two told what had happened on the way, and how Jesus was recognised by them when he broke the bread. (Luke 24.13–25)

1

The despairing journey

The final chapter of Luke's Gospel contains a story of great beauty and power in which the risen Christ is revealed to two despairing disciples who are in the process of retreating from the scenes of their devastated faith and hope in the city of Jerusalem. The attractiveness of this story is seen in the way in which it has repeatedly formed the subject matter of the great artists. Caravaggio painted the moment of recognition at the inn at Emmaus twice, depicting it as 'a jaw-dropping, napkin-spilling epiphany'; Rubens followed suit, while Rembrandt returned to this narrative many times and depicted it with unforgettable images.[1]

Of course, readers are liable to see different things in a narrative like this according to the historical and cultural context within which they read the text. Our particular situation shapes the kind of questions we bring to the story. It is, as already indicated, a story concerning the *resurrection* and readers familiar with the Bible therefore read it in the light of their knowledge of the revelation of the risen Christ which comes at its conclusion. We know the end of the story; indeed we can place this narrative within a wider context concerning the dynamic and joyful faith of the early Church that the Lord *had risen indeed.*

The danger here is that the context within which this revelation takes place may easily be overlooked. When the story begins there is absolutely no hint of the glory that will break into the darkness at its end. Indeed, the despair and utter hopelessness of the two disciples who withdraw from Jerusalem can hardly be exaggerated: both their body language and their conversation are symptoms of people deeply depressed and traumatized by suffering. Their faces, we are told, were 'downcast', and their emotional and spiritual condition is reflected in the telling phrase 'we had hoped'.

I want to suggest that in order to really hear what this story is saying our first move must be one in which we attempt to block out the knowledge we may possess of the 'happy ending' and imagine the situation of these two lonely people as they began their walk on the Emmaus road. What was their state of mind before the mysterious stranger drew up alongside them? In other words, we must simply begin at the beginning as 'two of them' start out 'to a village called Emmaus, about seven miles from Jerusalem'. We need to be willing to engage in an act of imagination that places us alongside these broken people as they retreat to the countryside, escaping from the scene of the holocaust that has shattered their faith in God and his Messiah and left them facing a future without horizons.

When we begin at this point, then this familiar narrative starts to resonate afresh in our contemporary historical and cultural situation. Millions of people in our world at the start of the third millennium find themselves walking a pathway that brings them very close to the lonely two on the road to Emmaus. Our world is full of people walking *away* from Jerusalem in despair with the words 'we had hoped' on their lips. Our times are actually defined in all kinds of ways as being *after* the ages of faith and hope; we are *post*-modern, *post*-Christian, even, it sometimes seems, *post*-human. In a world like this we must read this text where the storyteller begins, which means being absolutely honest and realistic about the experience of loss and desolation before we contemplate the possibility of a new beginning.

Christian mission, and in particular the practice of evangelism, has often ignored the order I am suggesting here, wanting to reverse the sequence in this story by beginning at the end, declaring the triumph of the resurrection without listening to the indications of pain, doubt and anger of those who have turned away from Jerusalem. The result is that the message declared by Christians is simply *unbelievable* for people whose emotional and spiritual experience renders them incapable of receiving such a message while their gaping wounds still require healing.

Actually, the story as it is told by Luke is completely true to psychological and spiritual reality: the Emmaus two simply could not receive the news of the risen Christ without first having grieved the loss of their previous dreams and hopes and passed through the dark night of the soul represented by their retreat from Jerusalem. At the start of the journey their emotional state made it impossible for them to recognize and receive the divine newness that was even then breaking into history through the risen Christ. It is precisely for this reason that he comes to them incognito, engaging them in a conversation that offers them space to bring to the surface the deep hurts that required open expression. And even at the end of the story there is no blaze of glory, but a revelation related to the most ordinary things as Christ becomes known in the deeply significant, symbolic act of breaking bread. He meets the despairing and hopeless couple *where they are* and simply walks beside them.

The lessons for us in all of this are multiple and we shall seek to explore them in detail later in this book. For now I want simply to highlight the fact that the story suggests the need for a revolutionary transformation of Christian witness in a broken and hurting world. Is it really too much to ask that Christians learn from the one they profess to follow what it means to 'come up and walk along with' people who are heading away from Jerusalem? What is implied here is the need to gain a true and empathetic understanding of the *context* within which people live their lives. In the Lukan narrative the mysterious stranger merely asks, 'What are you discussing together as you walk along?', so creating space within which his companions can unburden their hearts. By contrast, evangelism that begins with the declaration of glory is in danger of presenting dogmatic answers without reference to the real existential questions that people moving away from Jerusalem are asking. As the Canadian theologian Douglas John Hall has said, the first step towards a meaningful articulation of the Christian message in our modern context requires that churches 'become spheres of truth, places where people can give expression to the anxiety of meaninglessness and emptiness – without being utterly debilitated by the experience' (Hall, 2003, 131). He goes on to argue that the greatest theological task of our times is to articulate a fresh understanding of the meaning of 'salvation' that will actually speak to the pain and trauma of a generation that finds itself on the Emmaus road.

We had hoped

This pregnant phrase points back to the unfulfilled dreams and shattered hopes that have precipitated the flight from the city. As they make their way westwards, the setting sun seems to mirror the experience of the Emmaus walkers, as though nature itself is in sympathy with those whose faith and hope has turned to dust and ashes. In conversation with their uninvited companion, they describe how some of their colleagues had investigated a claim by a group of women that the crucified Jesus had returned to life, but the doleful conclusion is: 'him they did not see'. This suggests that in the aftermath of the traumatic events surrounding the execution of their leader, rumours and conspiracy theories multiplied. But the rumours that God might still be alive seem to the travellers on the road to be irrational and groundless, merely rubbing salt into already agonizing wounds. These are people for whom hope is exhausted and life itself begins to teeter on the brink of the abyss of meaninglessness. In such a situation the walk to Emmaus is a route out of madness, a retreat from a reality that has literally become unbearable, and the beginning of a quest for a way of coping with life in the absence of the old, familiar faith.

We will return to the causes of the despair of these particular walkers later, but here I want to consider some of the specific ways in which their experience is mirrored in the lives of people today. The modern world is full of people who for a variety of reasons are walking away from the tradition of Jerusalem. Indeed, the culture of modernity, having removed religion from the public sphere and made it a matter of purely private choice, might be described as an attempt to make human life meaningful and happy on the Emmaus road. We could say that the Enlightenment vision treated withdrawal from the 'tradition of Jerusalem' as a precondition for human happiness and well-being. Religious believers would be tolerated as, within the confines of their church buildings, they affirmed faith in God and prayed for a future in which awareness of the transcendent would be recovered within Western culture. But the intellectuals who led the great revolution of modern times felt no need to lament the removal of God from the public sphere. Indeed, the loss of the Father in heaven seemed to provide an open road towards an unprecedented re-creation of the world. Departing from Jerusalem following the presumed death of God, humanists believed that the road ahead offered a space within which human beings might at last come of age and take full responsibility for the world.

All of that now seems to have happened a long time ago. Very quickly the sun began to set over the road that led away from Jerusalem and it is not difficult to find humanists who lament the manner in which their particular dream of a new and transformed world has turned to ashes. In a series of profound studies the philosopher Leszek Kowlakowski has said,

> After centuries of the growth of the Enlightenment, we suddenly woke up in mental and cultural disarray; we are more and more frightened in the face of a world that is losing its religious legacy, and our fear is well justified. The lost myths seem to be replaced less by enlightened

7

rationality and more by terrifying secular caricatures and substitutes.

(Kowlakowski, 1990, 106–7)

This is a poignant statement which, with its language of 'fear' and 'terror', seems to echo the laments of the walkers to Emmaus. In Europe (both East and West) and in North America many thoughtful people, nurtured and educated within the Enlightenment worldview, now look at the dismal state of contemporary culture and find themselves saying: *we had hoped.* The sense of loss and betrayal can be found in the literature, art and music of our times as gifted people reflect on the consequences of the erosion of a secure and agreed basis for understanding what it means to be a human person. Jeremy Seabrook, in an unusual study of the impact of age-ing on the population of the world, suggests that the condi-tion of elderly people prompts a central question which many had thought laid to rest by the global triumph of industrial society, namely: 'Is the creation of more wealth synonymous with the betterment of human lives?' Are vulnerable people really helped by perpetually rising incomes, 'or does the cre-ation of wealth itself militate against social cohesion, belong-ing and solidarity?' (Seabrook, 2003, 51). Such profound questions, involving a critical examination of some of the fun-damental assumptions of modern culture, are increasingly raised by thoughtful people. Classical humanists with a strong moral and ethical sense are aware of the gathering darkness on the road to Emmaus and, in a world increasingly filled with 'secular substitutes and caricatures', find themselves isolated as their once dominant position in the West becomes an increasingly distant memory.

Christians can react to this in a number of ways, but I wish to suggest that as they also find themselves struggling to come to terms with painful endings and a time of massive uncer-tainty, they may begin to discover more in common with humanists than they imagined possible. These two traditions, long understood as polar opposites and divided by a kind of civil war that prevented both sides from recognizing their historical connections, have become companions on the Emmaus road. Might it be that their shared sense of lost visions and an uncertain future creates a context in which an honest dialogue can take place? Kowlakowski draws attention to the historic connections between these two traditions, but warns that once humanism turned atheistic and anti-Christian it obliterated all traces of its real origins and then removed the necessary limits on our freedom to determine good and evil. The result, he says, is that we find ourselves 'in a moral void' in which human beings, instead of becoming truly free and happy, are treated 'like instruments to be manipulated' (Kowlakowski, 1990, 29). Such an outcome is as distressing and worrying to the ethical humanist as it is to the Christian and so forms the starting point for conversation between them.[2]

New companions on the road

If Christians and humanists find themselves drawn together on the road to Emmaus, they may encounter other travellers on that pathway who bring their own distinctive contribution to the discussion. There is an obvious sense in which, as a matter of simple historical fact, Muslims are people who have 'turned away from Jerusalem', particularly from the 'tradition of Jerusalem' which identifies that city as the place where the drama of human redemption reached its climax in the crucifixion of Jesus of Nazareth. Like the Emmaus walkers, Muslims have found that story too hard to bear and while Jerusalem continues to play a central role within their own traditions, it no longer acts as *the* focal point for faith and devotion, since that is now located elsewhere. With the rejection of Muhammad's prophetic status by the Jews of Medina in AD 622, his followers ceased turning towards Jerusalem in prayer and redirected their devotions to the sacred city of Mecca which became, in both a literal and a symbolic sense, the point of Islam. One of the great attractions of this religion is its ability to create an extraordinary sense of belonging to a global community which, despite all its ethnic and racial diversity, finds its unity in this concentration on a single centre. Muslims have described themselves as 'the people of the point' and this focus on the centre is constantly reinforced both by ritual prayers, in which local congregations are linked 'like dots on the spokes of concentric wheels, on the single axis of the founding city', and through the experience of pilgrimage to that city in the annual Hajj, when the spokes 'become converging lanes of travel to a single rendezvous' (Cragg, 1978, 7).

However, despite this massive unity, and what can sometimes appear to outsiders to be an almost cast-iron certainty about matters of faith, many Muslims are to be found on the road to Emmaus with their own reasons for saying: *we had hoped*. In fact, Islam has always had its own deeply spiritual souls who have longed for an intimate communion with God that would transcend the mere performance of external rituals and the verbal confession of faith. Take this prayer, for example, which Constance Padwick discovered in one of the many Muslim prayer manuals she studied in the Middle East:

> I have naught but my destitution
>> To plead for me with Thee.
> And in my poverty I put forward that destitution as my
>> plea.
> I have no power save to knock at Thy door,
>> And if I be turned away, at what door shall I knock?
> Or on whom shall I call, crying his name,
>> If Thy generosity is refused to Thy destitute one?
> Far be it from Thy generosity to drive the disobedient
>> one to despair!
> Generosity is more free-handed, graces wider, than that.
> In lowly wretchedness I have come to Thy door,
>> Knowing that degradation there finds help.

In full abandon I put my trust in Thee,
    Stretching out my hands to Thee, a pleading beggar.
        (Munajatu 'l-Imani'sh-Shafii, in Padwick, 1961, 218)

People whose prayers are characterized by such profound humility and spiritual hunger are liable to be acutely aware of the gap that invariably seems to open up between the promise of religion and its actual practice, especially in situations where faith is linked to political and military power. What was promised, what people *had hoped for*, the creation of a world from which the idols that mislead and destroy human beings would be expelled and where justice would be established in human society, that great dream seems to be forever postponed, sometimes suffering almost total eclipse in a world in which the river of human tears is too often swollen by terrifying storms of suffering and violence. In such a world it is perhaps not so surprising that we hear Muslim voices, like that of Khurshid Ahmad from Pakistan, pleading for a recognition of the common, human concerns that demand dialogue as we walk together:

> Islam and the Western world today once again seem to be in a position to approach each other on a moral and ideological plane and, as such, be a source of strength to each other in a common struggle against those forces destined to destroy human civilization.
> (Quoted in Chapman, 1998, 193)[3]

Notice that this Muslim scholar identifies 'the Western world' as the dialogue partner for Islam today. That world, as we have seen, includes both Christians and humanists, who find themselves in a context in which old certainties are eroded and centuries of mutual hostility are being replaced by a shared concern for the future of humankind and for the beautiful planet we share together. If sensitive and humane Muslims share those concerns and wish to join the conversation on the Emmaus road, we must surely rejoice that our dialogue now

11

becomes a trialogue. And as we walk and talk together on that road, who knows but that we shall be joined by Another whose presence, now as then, can transform the conversation.

A final thought before we move on. Our story identifies one of the original walkers on the road as 'Cleopas', but it leaves his companion unidentified, nameless, anonymous. Given the importance of names in the ancient world we might draw negative conclusions from this detail; here is a literal nobody whose role in a story that has shaped the culture of the West remains unrecognized because his name was overlooked and forgotten! But perhaps by virtue of that very fact this person represents 'everyman'. Elsewhere in the Gospels, in one of the most wonderful of all the marvellous stories he told, Jesus is asked how we should define the term 'neighbour'. He responds by describing a man who is attacked and beaten, stripped naked and left speechless, yet despite losing all the recognized external signifiers of race or religion, he is embraced by a despised Samaritan who insists on recognizing as a neighbour any human person in need. Perhaps then the nameless walker on the road to Emmaus serves to remind us that anyone may join this conversation and that we should be open to companionship with all who feel alienated, disappointed and confused in the gathering gloom of a world growing old.

Dispatches from the Emmaus road

Name: Albert Camus

Biographical information: French philosopher, novelist and playwright. Born 1913 in Algeria, winner of the Nobel Prize for Literature in 1957, died in a road accident in 1960. He wrestled with the apparent 'absurdity' of a world in which human beings have an ineradicable craving for meaning, yet find themselves thrown into a universe that has become empty and silent. Few modern writers have expressed this dilemma with such clarity, honesty and courage; Camus writes from the Emmaus road.

> If one believes in nothing, if nothing makes sense, if we can assert no value whatsoever, everything is permissible and nothing is important. There is no pro or con; the murderer is neither right nor wrong. One is free to stoke the crematory fires, or to give one's life to the care of lepers. Wickedness and virtue are just accident or whim. (Camus, 1971, 13)[4]

> When the throne of God is overthrown, the rebel realizes that it is now his own responsibility to create the justice, order, and unity that he sought in vain within his own condition and, in this way, to justify the fall of God . . . This cannot come about without appalling consequences of which we are only, so far, aware of a few. (1971, 31)

> When man submits God to moral judgement, he kills him in his own heart. And then what is the basis of morality? God is denied in the name of justice but can the idea of justice be understood without the idea of God? Have we not arrived at absurdity? (1971, 57)

> All morality becomes provisional. The nineteenth and twentieth centuries, in their most profound manifestations, are centuries which have tried to live without transcendence. (1971, 112)

> Cynicism, the deification of history and of matter, individual terror and State crime, these are the inordinate

consequences that will now spring, armed to the teeth, from the equivocal conception of a world which entrusts to history alone the task of producing both values and truth . . . The sky is empty, the earth is delivered into the hands of power without principles. (1971, 116–17)

In contrast to the ancient world, the unity of the Christian and Marxist world is astonishing. The two doctrines have in common a vision of the world which completely separates them from the Greek attitude. Jaspers defines this very well: 'it is a Christian way of thinking to consider that the history of man is strictly unique'. (1971, 157)

How to live without grace – that is the question that dominates the nineteenth century. 'By justice' answered all of those who did not want to accept absolute nihilism. To the people who despaired of the Kingdom of Heaven, they promised the kingdom of men. The preaching of the city of humanity increased in fervour up to the end of the nineteenth century when it became really visionary in tone and placed scientific certainties in the service of Utopia. But the kingdom has retreated into the distance, gigantic wars have ravaged the oldest countries in Europe, the blood of rebels has bespattered walls, and total justice has approached not a step nearer. The question of the twentieth century . . . has gradually been specified: how to live without grace and without justice? (1971, 192)

I don't know whether this world has a meaning that transcends it. But I know that I do not know that meaning and that it is impossible for me just now to know it . . . And these two certainties – my appetite for the absolute and for unity and the impossibility of reducing this world to a rational and reasonable principle – I also know that I cannot reconcile them. (Camus, 1975, 51)[5]

[I]n the presence of God there is less a problem of freedom than a problem of evil. You know the alternative: either we are free and God the all-powerful is responsible for evil. Or we are free and responsible but God is not all powerful. All the scholastic subtleties have neither added anything nor subtracted anything from the acuteness of this paradox. (1975, 55)

The certainty of a God giving meaning to life far surpasses in attractiveness the ability to behave badly with
impunity. The choice would not be hard to make. But
there is no choice and that is where the bitterness comes
in. (1975, 65)

[T]he world needs real dialogue . . . falsehood is just as
much the opposite of dialogue as is silence, and . . . the
only possible dialogue is the kind between people who
remain what they are and speak their minds. This is
tantamount to saying that the world of today needs
Christians who remain Christians . . . I shall not try to pass
myself off as a Christian in your presence. I share with
you the same revulsion from evil. But I do not share your
hope and I continue to struggle against this universe in
which children suffer and die. (Camus, 1961, 50)

2

Christians on the Emmaus road

In the previous chapter I suggested that the biblical story of the Emmaus walk is capable of resonating today with many people who are *not* Christians and that, for this reason, it points us towards certain fundamental principles that should shape the nature and practice of Christian engagement with people in a secular culture. We will return to this point later, but here I wish to explore the significance of the fact that Christians across the Western world are themselves confronting a crisis of faith that may leave them uttering the cry of the Emmaus two: *we had hoped*.

In other words, the context in which we find ourselves today is not one in which Christians can approach unbelievers to offer answers to contemporary dilemmas as though they themselves are free from doubt and uncertainty. On the contrary, the fact that believers are thrown into a historical situation in which many of their inherited assumptions and certainties appear to be crumbling creates an opportunity for the kind of genuine dialogue we have heard a humanist writer like Albert Camus requesting. Christians cannot approach such conversations as people of massive strength and untroubled confidence, but rather as those who are also wounded and have their own unresolved dilemmas. When this is admitted then there is an opportunity for true companionship, replicating something like the experience of the Emmaus two who 'talked and discussed these things with each other' in the fading light of the evening.

Christianity in crisis

On the face of it a cultural context in which there is a widespread sense of malaise may sound like a golden opportunity for Christians to share with other people a story offering forgiveness, healing, hope and life. In periods of grave socio-cultural crisis in the past the Christian message has connected with the perceived needs of society in a way that has sparked movements of spiritual renewal and resulted in mass conversions. But although some Christians profess to discern the beginnings of just such a revival movement today, all the evidence suggests that the faith that has shaped the West for more than a thousand years has increasingly lost critical contact with the culture of the modern world.

I write these lines in Glasgow, one of the first great cities to emerge at the time of the industrial revolution. From my window I look out on a skyline dotted with the steeples and spires that reflect the response of Victorian Christianity to urbanization in the form of a massive programme of church-building. Today these buildings bear witness neither to spiritual vitality nor to the existence of a prophetic faith, but rather to the decline of faith in the city. When the window is open I hear the constant hum of traffic from a motorway that bisects the city and links it to Scotland's other great urban centre in Edinburgh. A few miles to the east, a church building perched on a hillside close to the motorway has for months displayed a large banner appealing to the thousands who pass it every day: SAVE THIS LANDMARK. Surely those who dreamed up this programme of restoration could not have noticed the tragic double irony in their slogan: the church reduced to a landmark, pleading with the world for salvation.[1]

This might serve as a parable concerning the state of Western Christianity. Recent research has suggested that churches in England are losing members at a rate that can be likened to 'a haemorrhage akin to a burst artery'. The same research warned that the familiar, institutional forms of Christianity 'are one generation from extinction' (Brierley,

2000, 236). How has this situation come about? How is it that Christianity, once a force shaping cultures across the Western world, is now so numerically reduced and socially and culturally marginalized?

Let us return for a moment to the illustration used above. If I continue my drive down the motorway past the church requesting a secular population to help preserve its fabric, I end up in the city of Edinburgh. There, less than a century ago, the first ecumenical missionary conference of modern times took place in a spirit of hope and optimism, expressed by the triumphalist slogan 'The evangelization of the world in this generation'. 'Edinburgh 1910' represented the floodtide of Western missionary optimism as Christians, confident in the superior nature of their civilization, 'lived in the intoxication of the certainty of victory' (Bosch, 1975, 50). They categorized the world as either 'Christian' or 'non-Christian', as 'evangelized' or 'non-evangelized', and were confident that, from a solidly Christian base, they stood on the brink of a golden age in which the technical, scientific and economic resources available within the 'Christian world' all but guaranteed the rapid conquest of the nations.

One of the key players at the Edinburgh conference was J. H. Oldham. In the following years, as the dreams of global missionary success were overwhelmed by the nightmares of the bloody conflict that devastated Europe, Joe Oldham reflected on the lessons of the times and concluded that the vision of missionary success that had inspired the Edinburgh conference had been seriously mistaken. In a statement that reveals prophetic insight, he wrote:

> I cannot help thinking that the war is teaching us to draw a clearer distinction . . . between the Church of Christ and what we have been accustomed to speak of as Christian civilization. We have assumed that we had a 'Christian civilization' which was something we could proudly offer to the non-Christian world. God is showing us how rotten that civilization is. We shall need in

the future to be more humble, to be more ready to take up the cross, follow Christ, and bear his reproach among men.

(Oldham, quoted in Clements, 1999, 140)

What Oldham had realized was that a Christianity in touch with its original sources would need to develop a far more *critical* engagement with the culture of the Western world than had been the case during the nineteenth century, and that, in doing so, it would find itself relocated away from the centre in new and unfamiliar territory at the margins of society. In the process of rediscovering a prophetic stance towards their own culture Christians would find that the language of loss and suffering which permeates the New Testament would begin to come alive. As Oldham's biographer notes, the experience of the war convinced him that the concept of the 'Christian nation' was bankrupt and that Western Christianity, while still sending thousands of missionaries overseas, 'had all but lost its credibility and its moral authority for engaging in such an enterprise' (Clements, 1999, 135).

It has taken almost one hundred years for these profound insights to become widely recognized as providing a true understanding of the position of Christians in relation to the culture of the modern Western world. Throughout the twentieth century the majority of believers in Europe and North America continued to regard their cultures as compatible with the message of the gospel and therefore as basically hospitable environments in which to follow Christ. The 'suffering church' was understood to be a distant reality located in Eastern Europe and China where evil, godless political systems were in control, so that the language of the Gospels concerning the cost of discipleship had little practical relevance to being Christian in Britain and the United States of America. Indeed, as far as the latter is concerned, a significant sociological study of American churches in the mid-twentieth century concluded that membership of such groups did not require the acceptance of a set of values at variance with those governing the wider society, but rather created 'a stronger and more explicitly religious affirmation of the same values held by the community at large' (Berger, 1961, 41). In other words, the assumption that the culture remained basically 'Christian' continued to operate throughout the twentieth century, and evidence to the contrary could be accommodated within this ruling paradigm by resorting to the idea that one more great evangelistic push, or a future 'revival', would restore 'business as usual' for the churches. The reality was otherwise since, by a process of what has been called 'religious inoculation', the vast majority of those who joined churches deeply embedded within the wider culture were 'effectively immunized against any real encounter with the Christian message' (1961, 116).

It is only now, with the churches of Europe greying and emptying, and those in North America detecting the beginnings of a major recession from Christian allegiance, that the reality of our situation becomes all but inescapable. Looking back on the twentieth century Christians across the Western world surely find themselves saying, 'We had hoped':

- We *had* hoped that the Great Commission would finally be completed.
- We *had* hoped that the mass evangelism of a gifted orator like Billy Graham would turn the tide of secularism and create the basis for a new era of Christian social dominance.
- We *had* hoped that the Charismatic movement would buck the trend of secularization and that the 'new churches' would fulfil their promises of bringing a restoration of former glories.
- We *had* hoped that the coming of AD 2000 would stimulate renewed evangelistic fervour and, after a 'decade of evangelism', we could face the new millennium with renewed confidence and joy.

But none of this has happened; the decline has not been arrested and we are left facing the real prospect of ecclesiastical meltdown. In this situation it should not be difficult for us to empathize with the two disciples on the Emmaus road.

21

Discovering who we are

In a situation like the one I have described we do well to turn away from the endless search for ways and means to recover the ground that has been lost and focus instead on the *theological* questions concerning what God might be doing through these events. In the Bible God is frequently described as bringing about the end of human social and religious arrangements that stand in the way of his purposes in the world, only for those terminations to become the ground on which startling new beginnings come to light.

In fact, this pattern of change and transition is to be found not only in Scripture but throughout the history of the Christian movement. We can trace it across the centuries in processes of expansion and decline in which a once dynamic and virile faith has repeatedly grown old and died, only to reappear in a different cultural context and in new forms. Perhaps nobody has expressed the importance of allowing what has grown old to die away better than Paul Tillich, who over fifty years ago observed that what is really new in history comes 'only in the moment when the old becomes visible *as* old and tragic and dying, and when no way out is seen'. With great insight Tillich recognized that what is truly new cannot be devised or constructed by us at all: 'All we can do is to be ready for it. We must realize as profoundly as possible that the former things have to become old, that they destroy our period just when we try most courageously to preserve the best of it' (Tillich, 1962, 183). Or, to express this in biblical language, there are times when judgement 'begins with the family of God' (1 Peter 4.17), because a once virile faith, gone to seed and serving ideologies that subvert the truth shown in Christ, has to be removed as a precondition for the emergence of the genuinely new things that God creates.

Has to be removed: that phrase has a deeply disturbing ring to it! It implies the necessity of loss and pain as the very foundations of our received traditions are shaken and much that is hallowed and beloved crumbles into dust. It suggests that we who have been accustomed to thinking only in terms of growth, expansion and success are called to live through recession, decline and failure, and that nothing we can do will alter this situation. For Western Christians, perhaps especially for North American believers, reared in a culture 'determinedly fixed upon the utter meaningfulness of our entire exercise in progress, in happiness', the entrance into such darkness is likely to be extremely difficult. And yet, as Douglas John Hall points out, only as we are willing to plumb the depths of the human predicament, to enter into the darkness of a world where hopes are dashed and the language of assured triumph dies upon our lips, only then is there likely to emerge a response to the anxiety of our times from the very depths of the Christian gospel (Hall, 2003, 131).

The sense that Christians in the West are themselves walking on the Emmaus road is heightened by the fact that we are currently passing through a period of *multiple endings*. It is not just that we face the struggle involved in the transition from modernity to the culture of the post-modern (a struggle in which, incidentally, humanists are also engaged), but rather that something far older than this, stretching back across many centuries, is coming to an end. Traditions of Christianity with roots that lie deep in the past seem to be withering away as the memory of the God of the Bible fades from the collective consciousness of entire peoples and the story of the gospel is lost in an act of collective amnesia.

At the risk of becoming boring, let me refer once more to the view from my office window. Just across the road from here is a rather beautiful area of old Glasgow which includes the ancient cathedral and a remarkable burial ground known as the Necropolis. In the tree-lined square in front of the cathedral stands a statue of the great Scottish missionary hero David Livingstone. I ask my students each year to cross the road and walk round that statue, noting the side panels depicting aspects of Livingstone's life, including his passionate opposition to slavery. But I then suggest that they look around the square and identify other statues, especially one located high above them, looking down from the side wall of the city's main hospital. Here, seated in appropriate pomp and glory, is the ubiquitous Queen Victoria, raised above Livingstone and dominating the scene.

Those two statues, one raised above the other, illustrate the ambiguities of the missionary movement which came into existence and expanded across the globe at precisely the time at which Europe extended its political and economic control around the world. Thus, when in 1904 the newly founded Sudan United Mission moved into Northern Nigeria it could do so only with the permission of the colonial authorities, and its personnel reported that they had difficulty communicating with local people who found it impossible to distinguish 'between flags, guns, tax collectors and bearers of the gospel message'. Little wonder then that the late Edward Said, in his seminal book *Orientalism*, saw a connection between Christian missionary activity and the manner in which Western discourse in general was a tool of colonialism and imperialism.[2]

But let us return to that square across the road: once my students have reflected on the relationship between the two statues, I ask them to enter the cathedral and make their way down to the crypt. Here they discover a memorial to nine Covenanting Christians who were hanged and beheaded at Glasgow Cross in 1684 and, moving back to even more remote times, the tomb of St Kentigern, the patron saint of Glasgow, better known as St Mungo. At this point real imagination is required in order to enter a totally different, pre-modern world in which life moved at a fraction of the pace symbolized by the nearby motorway. Here in the half-light of the crypt, we are transported back through time and are forcibly reminded of the kaleidoscopic variety of forms that the Christian movement has taken across the centuries. As the students sit in the quietness and semi-darkness of that ancient crypt, I ask them to reflect on what it is that connects *their* profession of faith in Christ to that of the Victorian missionaries, the Scottish martyrs brutally executed in the 'killing times' of the seventeenth century, and the Celtic saint who died around AD 612. The question becomes further complicated when they learn that the tomb before them became a major focus of pilgrimage in the medieval period and that among its notable visitors was King Edward I, who knelt before it on no less than three occasions in AD 1301. Many questions surface in the aftermath of such an experience: Is there any coherence to Christianity across the centuries, and if so, what is it that creates an underlying unity in the context of such a profusion of forms and expressions? But, more directly related to our concerns here is the question: Is this entire tradition, with all its variety and richness, about to be lost?

It seems to me that the confusion and uncertainty felt by Western Christians today is related precisely to the fact that what is under threat is not some limited, local tradition, but rather the entire Western Christian heritage in all its variety and antiquity. As Stuart Murray has written, the immediate future is likely to be a very difficult time for Christians 'in a society that has rejected institutional Christianity and is familiar enough with the Christian story not to want to hear it again'. In this situation almost all our inherited assumptions concerning the nature of the Church and its calling are likely to prove inadequate, if not actually misleading. However, as Murray says, if Christians can 'face into this future rather than hankering after a fading past', if they 'resist short-term packages and pre-packaged answers' and learn how to be cross-cultural missionaries in a secular society, then 'whatever culture emerges from the ruins of Christendom might offer tremendous opportunities for telling and living out the Christian story in a society where this is largely unknown' (Murray, 2004, 8).

Which brings us back again to the Emmaus walkers who, the text informs us, had been hoping that the prophet Jesus 'was going to redeem Israel'. That is to say, prior to the devastating events in Jerusalem, they had come to believe that the crucial turning point in human history had arrived. The rule of tyrants was about to be ended and the long-hoped-for reign of God was about to be established. They themselves would be in the vanguard of a movement that would witness the restoration of the honour and glory of God and the ethical and moral transformation of the world. Language of this kind is not so far removed from that heard at the Edinburgh conference in 1910 when, as we have seen, Christians entertained hopes for the missionary conquest of the world. But this hope, which theologians have come to describe as a 'theology of glory', was soon overwhelmed by the tragedies of history, and the dreams of assured progress gave way to nightmares as the veneer of a Christian civilization was shattered by an unprecedented eruption of evil and violence. Theories of history which had treated Western civilization as the advance guard of a new, more highly developed species of humanity, and which had seemed to make perfect sense in the Victorian era, were suddenly exposed as the expression of a ridiculous hubris. To use a famous phrase, the lights went out across Europe and Christians joined others in lamenting: *we had hoped.*

I want to end this chapter by quoting a long poem by Dennis O'Driscoll which was published as 'The Saturday Poem' in the *Guardian* newspaper in December 2002:

Missing God
His grace is no longer called for
before meals: farmed fish multiply
without His intercession.
Bread production rises through
disease-resistant grains devised
scientifically to mitigate His faults.

Yet, though we rebelled against Him
like adolescents, uplifted to see
an oppressive father banished –
a bearded hermit – to the desert,
we confess to missing Him at times.

Miss Him during the civil wedding
when, at the blossomy altar
of the registrar's desk, we wait in vain
to be fed a line containing words
like 'everlasting' and 'divine'.

Miss Him when the TV scientist
explains the cosmos through equations,
leaving our planet to revolve on its axis
aimlessly, a wheel skidding in snow.

Miss Him when the radio catches a snatch
of plainchant from some echoey priory;
when the gospel choir raises its collective voice
to ask Shall We Gather at the River?
or the forces of the oratorio converge
on I Know That My Redeemer Liveth
and our contracted hearts lose a beat.

Miss Him when a choked voice at
the crematorium recites the poem
about fearing no more the heat of the sun.

Miss Him when we stand in judgement
on a lank Crucifixion in an art museum,
its stripe-like ribs testifying to rank.

Miss Him when the gamma-rays
recorded on the satellite graph
seem arranged into a celestial score,
the music of the spheres,
the Ave Verum Corpus of the observatory lab.

Miss Him when we stumble on the breast lump
for the first time and an involuntary prayer
escapes our lips; when a shadow crosses
our bodies on an x-ray screen; when we receive
a transfusion of foaming blood
sacrificed anonymously to save life.

Miss Him when we exclaim His name
spontaneously in awe or anger
as a woman in a birth ward
calls to her long-dead mother.

Miss Him when the linen-covered
dining table holds warm bread rolls,
shiny glasses of red wine.

Miss Him when a dove swoops
from the orange grove in a tourist village
just as the monastery bell begins to take its toll.

Miss Him when our journey leads us
under leaves of Gothic tracery, an arch
of overlapping branches that meet
like hands in Michelangelo's Creation.

Miss Him when, trudging past a church,
we catch a residual blast of incense,
a perfume on par with the fresh-baked loaf
which Milosz compared to happiness.

Miss Him when our newly-fitted kitchen
comes in Shaker-style and we order
a matching set of Mother Ann Lee chairs.

Miss Him when we listen to the prophecy
of astronomers that the visible galaxies
will recede as the universe expands.

Miss Him when the sunset makes
its presence felt in the stained glass
window of the fake antique lounge bar.

Miss Him the way an uncoupled glider
riding the evening thermals misses its tug.

Miss Him, as the lovers shrugging
shoulders outside the cheap hotel
ponder what their next move should be.

Even feel nostalgic, odd days,
for His Second Coming,
like standing in the brick
dome of a dovecote
after the birds have flown.[3]

Here, surely, is the authentic language of the Emmaus road experience, of those who tread a path from which God has *gone missing*, and yet confess that as the sky darkens and the air grows cold, they are *missing God*. It is the language of Nietzsche's famous 'madman' who, having discovered the divine absence that turned the churches of Europe into 'the tombs and sepulchres of God', realized that humankind was now 'perpetually falling', existing in 'an infinite nothing' with no 'up or down left' (Hollindale, 1977, 202–3). At such a time Christians will be able to communicate with those who are missing God only if they are willing to be absolutely honest concerning the sense of crisis and loss that brings them to the Emmaus road and makes them into genuine companions and partners on the journey. As the following 'Dispatch' suggests, the painful experience of the ending of Christendom may turn out to be a disguised blessing if it creates the space within which those who confess Jesus as the Christ are able to rediscover their true identity and regain a lost credibility that will enable them to join the conversation on the road.

Dispatches from the Emmaus road

Name: Jacques Ellul

Biographical information: French academic, born in Bordeaux in 1912. Became Professor of Law and the Sociology and History of Institutions at the University of Bordeaux. An active member of the French Resistance during World War Two, he was a prolific author with a particular interest in contemporary culture and what he saw as the negative impact of technology on human life. Influenced as a young man by the work of Karl Marx, he read widely in Christian theology and was a member of the French Reformed Church. His books, which have been translated into many languages, contain searching, critical analyses of Western Christianity, and have been seen by many as offering a prophetic contribution to modern thought. The titles from which the following quotations are drawn suggest that Ellul's voice offers a Christian contribution to the dialogue on the Emmaus road: *The Subversion of Christianity* (1986); *Hope in Time of Abandonment* (1973); and *The New Demons* (1975). Ellul died in 1994.

> How has it come about that the development of Christianity and the church has given birth to a society, a culture that are completely opposite to what we read in the Bible, to what is indisputably the text of the law, the prophets, Jesus and Paul? . . . There is not just deviation but radical and essential contradiction, or real subversion. (Ellul, 1986, 3)[4]

> Evangelical proclamation was essentially subversive. Put in danger by it, the forces of the social body have replied by integrating this power of negation, of challenge, by absorbing it through so disguising themselves that Christians thought there had been a social transformation . . . In reality, the social group that gave strong adherence to Christianity (the political, social and intellectual elite) brought with them a social ritual that was the exact opposite of what Jesus proclaimed. (1986, 21)

> Christendom has astutely abolished Christianity by making us all Christians . . . In Christendom there is not the

slightest idea of what Christianity is. People cannot understand that Christianity has been abolished by its propagation ... Christianity became what one might call the structural ideology of this particular society. It ceased to be an explosive ferment calling everything into question in the name of the truth that is in Jesus Christ, in the name of the incarnation. (1986, 36–9)

All that is left of Christianity is morality, a bourgeois morality with which everyone is familiar, and a few conventional ideas (the clergy have a role to play in society; the cathedrals are an attractive element of the civic scene). Post-Christian society therefore, is not simply a society that has followed upon Christendom. It is a society that is no longer Christian, a society that has had the experience of Christianity, is the heir of the Christian past, and believes that it has full knowledge of the Christian religion because it retains vague memories of it and sees remnants of it all around. (Ellul, 1975, 25)[5]

If the factual reality of modern man is [the] death of hope, the problem for theology is not the death of God but the silence of God. It is no longer: God is dead because man no longer believes in him; but rather: man is without hope because God is silent. Such is the basic spiritual reality of this age – God is turned away. God is absent. God is silent. (Ellul, 1973, 110–11)

We have created a world in which words proliferate, a world of 'news' that tells us nothing. We are living in a deluge of bulletins, in an uninterrupted verbal explosion. All is talk, all the time to all the world, and nothing is being said. In this flood of sound which comes at us, made up of endless repetition, empty curiosities, inner and intellectual vacuity, no word can really be a word. All is blended into an undifferentiated mishmash, in which scientific information is drowned in news flashes; or a crucial political decision is a headline alongside murders and auto accidents; or the most agonized human appeal is obliterated by the musical alcohol of pop and made the excuse for other kinds of talk to interest viewers; or a key statement is used to spice up a release.

No definitive word is any longer possible. There are no longer any final questions or answers. (1973, 123–4)

Nevertheless, Christ is there. The cross that is planted at the heart of the history of the world cannot be uprooted. The risen Christ is with us to the end of the world. The Holy Spirit acts in secret and with infinite patience. There is a church that is constantly born and reborn. (Ellul, 1986, 191)

The striking thing in the church's history is that through tremendous perversion, when everything seems to be eaten up by termites, there have always been resurgences of truth. (1986, 199)

Transformation of the church does not begin at its human head but with an explosion originating with those on the fringe . . . The reduction to the temporal and to power excludes meaning, and this leaves a large, gaping hole that we try in vain to fill, that cries out unceasingly until the eternal comes to fill it. In the course of history then, nothing is ever lost. Christianity never carries the day decisively against Christ. Christ may sometimes rest, even for long periods, as he was hidden in the body of that little Jewish man. (1986, 212)

3

The unknown Christ

We move now to consider the point in our narrative at which the two companions on the road are joined by an unknown stranger who comes uninvited and walks along with them. His enquiry concerning the topic of their conversation results in a dual response, part physical, part verbal, which makes it quite clear that the stranger's intervention was seen as an unwelcome intrusion into private grief. The physical reaction is described in the phrase, 'They stood still', which might be paraphrased in contemporary language as 'they were stopped dead in their tracks' – astounded and baffled by their new companion's unaccountable ignorance. This sense of astonishment, mixed with a rising feeling of anxiety concerning the identity and purpose of this mysterious person, is evident in the verbal response of Cleopas: 'Are you the only one living in Jerusalem who does not know the things that have happened there in these days?' There is a note of condescension bordering on contempt here and, reading between the lines, we discern a spirit of deep suspicion, confusion and fear.

Before we examine the stranger's response, I want to reflect in greater detail on the condition of the two disciples. The patient probing of the stranger, expressed in his supplementary question, 'What things?' releases a veritable flood of words as their pent-up grief is suddenly poured out in a confession of utter hopelessness. The narrative suggests profound depths of despair by its repeated use of past tenses (Jesus *'was* a prophet'; the disciples *'had* hoped') and negatives (they 'did *not* find his body'; him they 'did *not* see'). In their uninhibited lament the disciples make two particular statements that are revealing of the deepest causes of their confusion and despair.

Notice, first, their opening statement that their dead leader 'was a prophet'. We may understand this to mean either, very simply, that the prophetic career of Jesus, validated by the power of his words and deeds, had been cut tragically short by death; or the statement can be read as indicating that the terrible nature of Jesus' death by crucifixion now cast doubt upon his status as a prophet. Instead of being hailed as Messiah and acclaimed as Israel's saviour and liberator, he had been dismissed and treated as a deceiver and a traitor. Can the disgraced, dishonoured Jesus still be regarded as a true prophet, or is that belief now exposed as a delusion, a tragic error?

This really is a crucial question not just for the broken travellers on the road to Emmaus in the first century, but for those of us who discover ourselves facing similar dilemmas and uncertainties in the twenty-first century. If the first followers of Jesus found it difficult to reconcile their original belief in his prophetic status with the shattering experience of his disgraceful, horrible and very public death, Christians in later ages have experienced similar problems and have found various ways of reinterpreting that death so as to limit its offensiveness. In the centuries that followed the death of Jesus, his status as a prophet receded from view, eclipsed by categories that made him at one time omnipotent king, at another, cosmic Lord, and yet again, the lover of the individual soul. Such descriptions are not necessarily wrong in themselves since Christ cannot be contained within one set of titles; the tragedy is that descriptions focused on power, honour and glory have repeatedly overwhelmed and eclipsed the original identity of Jesus of Nazareth.

The relevance of this to our modern 'Emmaus dialogues' is clear when we note the observation of Jaroslav Pelikan in his brilliant study of the impact of Jesus on the history of culture, that by the time Islam burst upon the world in the seventh century claiming Jesus as a great prophet, Christians had forgotten that he was so described in the Gospels and actually condemned Muslims for using a title they now viewed as, at best, inadequate. Pelikan comments: 'Consequently, the potential significance of the figure of Jesus as a meeting ground between Christians and Jews, and between Christians and Muslims, has never materialized' (Pelikan, 1985, 17).

What if our modern Emmaus experience, as described earlier in this book, is bringing us into a context in which that potential might be realized as Christians, Jews and Muslims, in a world threatened by violence and terror as never before, attempt to break through the distortions and stereotypes of history and discuss together the significance of Jesus, the prophet?

Were this to happen there would be obvious questions that Christians would wish to ask their Jewish and Muslim friends. Islam, for example, has defined the role of the prophet in a manner that makes it easy for Muslims to sympathize with the travellers on the Emmaus road. The difficulty, the near impossibility, of squaring the term 'prophet' with a biography that ends in public humiliation and the terrible death of one who is branded as a criminal is something felt with peculiar force by Muslims. The problem is solved by denying that such an end to the life of Jesus ever occurred; there was no cross and no humiliation. But we may ask – in an age increasingly characterized by acts of terror in which religion is all too often implicated, we *must* ask – whether the removal of the crucified Messiah from human history leaves us confined within definitions of prophecy limited to categories involving honour and power, and whether, in that case, it is more or less likely that we can hope for a world beyond violence and domination.[1] As we shall ask later: what precisely is meant in our narrative when the stranger insists that the Messiah *had* to 'suffer these things'?

However, if Christians are to ask such questions, if they are to engage in such a dialogue with any credibility, they will need to overcome and repudiate those forms of their own religion which, as we have seen earlier, have involved the radical subversion of the message of Christ. As Jürgen Moltmann has said, a Christianity which once 'conquered the world' must now learn to 'conquer its own forms when they have become worldly'. The reformation required to achieve such a trans-formation will involve breaking down 'the idols of the Christian West' and, in radical way, remembering the 'crucified God' (Moltmann, 1974, 36).

This brings us to the second statement in our text in which the disciples reveal the deepest causes of their distress. They describe how the 'chief priests and our rulers handed him over to be sentenced to death, and they crucified him'. When, twenty centuries after the event, we read a text like this for devotional purposes, the historical context within which the things described took place may all too easily be lost from view. Jesus, the Galilean prophet, had fallen foul of the powers that be; his trial and execution were formal, judicial acts, which meant that both he and his followers were now branded as traitors. James Alison has well described the situation the followers of Jesus found themselves in after his execution as one in which, since they were easily identifiable in Jerusalem as 'foreigners', they were 'linked with a major criminal who had just been executed'. The paralysing fear that drives this group under-ground, meeting behind locked doors, and skulking away from Jerusalem under cover of darkness, now becomes entirely understandable. Alison is justified in describing the Jesus community in the immediate aftermath of his crucifixion, as 'a group of disillusioned, frightened, guilty, mournful semi-traitors' (Alison, 2005, 121). This also explains the ambivalence and uncertainty of our two walkers to Emmaus concerning their uninvited and unrecognized companion:

- Who is this person?
- Why is he so inquisitive?
- Is conversation with him likely to be incriminating?

The tables turned

This brings us to the words of the stranger. His opening statement is surprising, perhaps puzzling, in that instead of offering soothing, comforting words, he makes what (to

Western ears at least) seems to be a direct and somewhat blunt accusation of responsibility: 'How foolish you are . . .' In other words, he suggests that they are, at least in part, culpable in relation to their despair and hopelessness. Their desperation stems ultimately from their acceptance of a fundamentally mistaken worldview which was based on a particular, and highly selective, reading of the Hebrew Scriptures. The statement made earlier in the account, that the travellers 'were kept' from recognizing Christ, thus means that their ignorance was due, not to some magical act of God, but to their own deeply mistaken reading of the Scriptures. Shaped by the culture to which they belonged, they had, in common with the rest of Jesus' followers, been misled by an ideological reading of the Bible. The interpretative tradition which underlay the hopes they had placed in the prophet Jesus was a false tradition. Consequently, what they had been hoping for was simply wrong. Despite being dressed up in sacred language, they had been trapped within a misleading and false ideology!

Suddenly the tables are being turned: the 'ignorant' stranger proves able to interpret the Scriptures in a way that begins to transform the situation, while the disciples' assumption that they are in full command of the facts is challenged and they are made aware of huge gaps in their knowledge.

What this conversation suggests is that the Emmaus road, while offering hope for the discovery of radical newness, does not provide us with what Dietrich Bonhoeffer famously called 'cheap grace'. Christ does not come with a therapy designed to suppress our pain, but with a searching and disturbing exposure of the extent to which we may bear responsibility for the misery of our condition. He does not offer comforting reassurance to the hopeless that it will all work out as expected in the end; rather he presents the challenge to consider whether our hope was well founded in the first place. Now, as then, it is often the case, as Krister Stendahl observes, that our vision is more likely to be obstructed 'by what we think we know than by our lack of knowledge' (Stendahl, 1976, 7). So, while the Emmaus road is indeed a healing place, it is so only as it first creates the space within which we can look again at what we thought we knew, and humbly recognize the partial nature of our previous understanding of the ways of God.

Delusions of grandeur

I want to dwell on the precise manner in which the walkers on the Emmaus road are challenged to face up to their responsibility for the loss of hope they have experienced. There are, I want to suggest, two crucial mistakes made by the disciples and both of these contain searching challenges for us today. First, the highly selective, culture-bound manner in which they had interpreted the prophetic writings resulted in a radical distortion of the hope contained within the Bible. This is the unmistakable implication of the stranger's charge that they had failed to believe '*all* that the prophets have spoken'. The Bible study that he proceeds to deliver is an obvious corrective to this distortion as, 'beginning with Moses and *all* the prophets', he expounds the teaching of '*all* the Scriptures concerning himself'.

Put briefly, the disciples had accepted definitions of terms like 'Messiah' and 'redemption' based on one stream of prophetic expectation, that which focused on the power, honour and glory of the messianic age. This tradition is clearly present within the Bible, but it exists there alongside and in tension with another, contrasting expectation of messianic suffering, rejection and death. The unrecognized stranger on the road points out that when these strands are properly related to each other it becomes clear that the Messiah cannot achieve the glory of the kingdom finally come without first experiencing pain, loss and humiliation. To do so, to seek to bring about the transformation of the world and establish the rule of justice and truth simply by the exercise of power, would be to take the route of 'normal' politics, so perpetuating never-ending cycles of violence and tragedy. In fact, the Hebrew Bible, when read without the distorting lenses of a narrow nationalism, promised a radically new way involving the Messiah's acceptance of suffering as the divine route to ultimate vindication and glory.

The question with which those of us who travel the 'Emmaus road' in the twenty-first century are here confronted concerns the unrecognized and unacknowledged ways in which our worldviews have distorted our understanding, so that the misery of our condition is traceable to a dangerous overconfidence concerning our grasp of truth and reality. I believe this to be an issue that must be faced honestly by all modern people, but I am especially concerned with the challenges confronting Christians at this point. Living amid the ruins of Christendom, they must ask themselves whether the darkness and pessimism that so often appears to characterize their present existence, particularly on the continent of Europe, may actually be the outcome of their own 'foolishness'. Too often, I suggest, as believers struggle to maintain the inherited institutional forms of the Christian religion, they are tempted to conclude that the source of the crisis is to be located 'out there'; it is the *world* that has gone adrift, while the Church remains in possession of the answers to contemporary dilemmas and traumas. Such assumptions frequently underlie both Protestant and Roman Catholic analyses of the condition of Western culture, as can be seen in the claim of Pope John Paul II that a united Europe requires a recovery of 'values that are most fully manifested in the Christian tradition' (John Paul II, 2003, 17).

But is that really the case? Have the Churches of Europe ordered their lives according to the values of the gospel? The voices from the modern Emmaus road to which we have listened earlier in this book suggest that the answer to that fundamental question is far from clear. The witness of history would seem to justify the devastating sentence with which Richard Niebuhr commenced his ground-breaking study of the divisions and factionalism of Western Christianity: 'Christendom has often achieved apparent success by ignoring the precepts of its founder.' He went on to demonstrate the ways in which the urge to make alliances with privilege and power had repeatedly resulted in the violation of the spirit of the gospel and concluded that the institutional church had found it easier to 'give to Caesar the things that belonged to Caesar' when 'what might belong to God was not too closely pressed' (Niebuhr, 1929, 3).

So then, the voice of the 'unknown Christ' echoes across the centuries, demanding that we re-examine the basis of our faded dreams and hopes and ask ourselves whether our present distress may not find its source in received models of the Church and its mission that are, in fact, based on a one-sided and highly selective interpretation of the Scriptures. Like the original Emmaus walkers we have repeatedly failed to believe 'all that the prophets have spoken', filtering out those elements of the tradition that summon us to radical conversion and call us into a community of men and women no longer in thrall to idols and liberated to live a new life in Christ. The issues that face us here involve more than simply a critical review of history; they compel us to ask how it is possible to be truly 'Christian' in an age when the technological, individualist, success-oriented culture of the Western world so clearly possesses the power to distort our reading of the Scriptures we profess to honour. Such subversion places us in grave danger of embracing a syncretism that offers a halo of sanctity to values and actions that are the antithesis of the model of human life under the reign of God revealed to us by Jesus of Nazareth.[2] In such a context the summons of the crucified Christ – that we recognize the foolishness of unbiblical dreams of power and glory, and repent of the ways in which we have distorted and misrepresented him before the world – comes to us as a word of grace, pointing towards a path leading out of our present darkness and towards the renewal of genuine hope. What this might mean in practice is well expressed by the Catholic theologian Johann Baptist Metz:

The crisis (or sickness) of the life in the church is not just that the change of heart is not taking place or not taking place quickly enough, but that the absence of this change of heart is being further concealed under the appearance of a merely *believed-in-faith.* Are we Christians ... really changing our hearts, or do we just believe in a change of hearts and remain under the cloak of this belief in conversion basically unchanged? Are we living as disciples, or do we just believe in discipleship and, under the cloak of this belief in discipleship, continue in our old ways, the same unchanging ways? Do we show real love, or do we just believe in love and under the cloak of belief in love remain the same egoists and conformists we have always been? Do we share the sufferings of others, or do we just believe in this sharing, remaining under a cloak of belief in 'sympathy' as apathetic as ever?

(Metz, 1981, 3)

Resuming the trialogue

I have suggested above how the searching questions posed by the anonymous Christ on the walk to Emmaus challenge contemporary Christians; do they also have something to say to their fellow-travellers on the modern Emmaus road? As long ago as 1851 Matthew Arnold described in 'Dover Beach' the 'melancholy, long, withdrawing roar' of the Sea of Faith and predicted that this would lead to a world with 'neither joy, nor love, nor light, Nor certitude, nor peace, nor help for pain'. Sensing that the tide had already begun to turn for religion in Europe, Arnold realized that this momentous development would have serious implications for the wider culture and, in memorable lines, he anticipated the 'Emmaus experience' we have attempted to describe in the foregoing pages:

> And we are here as on a darkling plain
> Swept with confused alarms of struggle and flight,
> Where ignorant armies clash by night.

The reference to 'ignorant armies' may be understood as both an anticipation of real, military conflicts (a prophecy all too tragically fulfilled), and a prediction of the looming clash of ideas as a shared vision of a transformed world was lost and Western culture became fragmented by deep and bitter ideological conflicts. The writer Philip Pullman has observed that it is perfectly possible to reject belief in God and retain what may be described as a 'theocratic mindset'. An obvious example of this is to be found in the former Soviet Union where official atheism was accompanied by the reverencing of a new set of sacred texts, the creation of 'secular saints' whose images were publicly venerated, and the establishment of an inquisitorial system designed to enforce absolute obedience and submission to officially decreed orthodox belief. Pullman describes the Soviet Union as 'one of the most thorough-going theocracies the world has ever seen' and concludes that, when Stalin's Russia is compared with Khomeini's Iran, it becomes obvious that belief in God is not the cause of the problem since 'the most dogmatic materialist is functionally equivalent to the most fanatical believer' (Pullman, 2004, 157).

All of which compels us to ask whether, on the 'darkling plain' on which we find ourselves today, contemporary humanists may not need to ask themselves whether the voice of the suffering Messiah, chiding human arrogance and the lust for power, is not addressed to them as well as to his professed followers.

- Is *their* grief and disillusion, and the temptation to a nihilism that endangers what is best in their own tradition, the outcome of an unrecognized foolishness?
- Can *they* now recognize that the positivist claim to have discovered an exclusive route to the understanding of reality is exposed by history as a dangerous delusion?
- And have *they* isolated one strand of the witness of the prophets, separating the love of neighbour from the love of God, and so substituting law for life, and endangering the spiritual faculty without which human flourishing appears to be impossible?

Even as these lines were being written, in the approach to Christmas 2005, I came across a remarkable article from a humanist source that confirmed my hunch that Christians today find themselves sharing the Emmaus road with people of good will from other traditions. Jenni Russell describes how her parents abandoned faith in the light of their experiences of forms of religion that 'provided no defence, no explanation and sometimes much justification for some of the worst horrors of the twentieth century'. Like many contemporary Western people, she inherited an assumption 'that there is something desirable about a secular, rather than a religious, approach to existence'. And yet, in the approach to Christmas, amid the consumerist onslaught that occurs with ever-increasing power, Russell encountered believers 'who feel real joy, awe and solemnity about the Christmas story and all it represents'. Despite her atheism she found herself deeply moved by the Christian message of peace, hope, love and redemption and discovered within herself a 'longing to feel that there is something above and beyond our own small desires that might give meaning to our lives'. Here is a self-critical humanism that is 'moving toward Emmaus':

> Here on earth [believers] are, on the whole, happier and longer-lived than the rest of us. Which leaves us non-believers with an uncomfortable problem. Is it just that we haven't found the language to inspire people as religion does, or does rationality have its limits? It seems to me that most of us wish there was a purpose in life beyond the mundane, and that there are aspects of life that rationality doesn't reach. The difficulty of being a secular believer in the potential goodness of man is that we keep running up against incontrovertible evidence of our own and everyone else's charmless failings. The depressing realization for those of us who don't have God to tell us to think of others is to discover that, in the absence of faith, people are more likely to turn to consumerism than humanism.
>
> (Russell, 2005)

Clearly, Christians and humanists may discover a common agenda here. And the same thing may be said of other traditions, including Muslims who, having reached the Emmaus road by a somewhat different route, have their own reasons to lament the fading of previous hopes and visions. In the gloom we experience together, and with a shared hope for the coming of a new world characterized by love and justice, perhaps Muslims also may hear afresh the voice of the prophet Isa and recognize that his charge of 'foolishness' has application in relation to their own traditions and expectations.

Voices from the margins

Earlier in this chapter I suggested that the Gospel story of the walk to Emmaus indicates that the crestfallen disciples were guilty of *two* fundamental mistakes that help to explain their misery and confusion. The first of these, the acceptance of an ideological reading of the Hebrew Scriptures, we have now explored at some length. Which brings us to the second mistake, which is to be found in their dismissal of the testimony of certain witnesses whose words were capable of transforming the situation.

In recounting to their unrecognized companion the events that had taken place in Jerusalem, the Emmaus walkers refer to the fact that 'some of our women' had claimed to have seen a vision of angels at the tomb of Jesus and that these extra-terrestrials had announced that Christ was alive! However, the women had not set eyes on the body of Jesus and when their stories were investigated by 'some of our companions' they found no genuine evidence to justify the women's visionary claims.

The two phrases, 'our women' and 'our companions' clearly indicate distinct social groups with contrasting levels of authority and credibility. The 'women' are marginal people whose testimony is automatically suspect and requires proper evaluation and sifting by those who possess recognized authority. Any doubts that this is a correct reading of the text are dispelled when we recall that Luke has earlier informed us that the apostles dismissed the women's testimony since 'their words seemed to them like nonsense' (24.11). There is no ambiguity here: the experience of women is by definition unreliable as the basis for determining what counts as reality and truth.

By contrast, the 'companions' are to be trusted; these are the recognized gatekeepers of knowledge who are able to distinguish between 'fact' and fantasy and their verdicts carry an authority that overrides the testimony of marginal people based on claims to visionary experience. The Emmaus two clearly defer to the verdict of the 'companions'; once they have spoken the issue is settled! The 'companions', having set out to investigate the facts, concluded that the empirical evidence confirmed the dismal message of the women that the body of the dead Christ had gone missing, while the rumours of angels and talk of resurrection are passed over as inadmissible to the investigation.

Are the Emmaus walkers not revealed here to be *doubly foolish*? Not only have they misread the Bible, they have failed to recognize and imitate the radical example of social transformation displayed before their own eyes in the life of Jesus. That example should have convinced them not simply that the voices of marginal people matter, but that truth is more likely to be understood and expressed by those who are despised and feared in the corridors of privilege and power. Why was the testimony of the women so summarily dismissed when it is a *female* voice which, on almost the first page of Luke's Gospel, announces that those who are 'proud in their inmost thoughts' will be 'scattered'? The same revolutionary song anticipates that the poor and humble, those who live on the margins, will be 'lifted up'. And indeed they are: Jesus creates a scandal by publicly accepting the devotion of a weeping woman 'who lived a sinful life', and declares that her experience of grace and forgiveness gave her access to a form of knowledge denied to the proud and self-confident. Elsewhere, a woman who breaks free from her defined domestic role and dares to take the position of a disciple at the feet of the Rabbi is said by Christ to have 'chosen what is better'. Widows are held up as examples of piety and generosity, and even small children become models for those who would enter this 'upside-down-kingdom'.

The conclusion is inescapable: when the Emmaus two gave precedence to the views of the 'companions' against the knowledge of the women, they betrayed the example of their Lord, accepted the normal criteria by which wisdom is defined and knowledge is understood, and condemned themselves to walk in a darkness unrelieved by the signs of hope that were in fact available to them.

Yet again the biblical narrative poses questions for us:

- Who are the gatekeepers of knowledge upon whom we rely and by what authority do they determine the limits of reality?
- Who are the marginalized people whose voices go unheard because it is assumed they know little that is of importance?
- And how might our perceptions of truth have become dangerously narrowed by a kind of myopia that blocks access to sources of knowledge and wisdom capable of enriching our lives and renewing our hope?

I wish to propose that for Western Christians on the modern Emmaus road, one vital source of wisdom is to be discovered today in the churches that exist outside the old, declining Christendom. These are churches that came to birth in areas of the world that were 'marginal' from the perspective of the metropolitan and imperial centres of power. In Chapter 2 we noticed the manner in which Western Christians viewed the world at the beginning of the twentieth century, identifying the vast continent of Africa, and the even more mysterious and remote regions of Asia, as the 'unevangelized' world in need of the knowledge and wisdom that providence had entrusted to civilized and Christianized nations. Now, with the collapse of such a simplistic worldview, and in the confusion and uncertainty of our modern 'Emmaus experience', Western believers find themselves in a radically changed context in which the 'centre' of the Christian movement has reappeared in what we thought were the 'margins'. And from those 'margins' voices are heard offering us new perspectives and fresh hope. There are 'rumours of angels' in a globalized world, but the question is (now as at the beginning) whether humble witnesses whose testimonies are capable of renewing hope, will be heard in the old centres of power and knowledge.

Actually, I suspect that there are deep, underlying and often unrecognized reasons why Western believers frequently fail to benefit from the insights offered to them from the new heartlands of the Christian movement. The voices from the 'margins' come from people who have learned of Christ and the gospel in contexts that are vastly different from that in which European Christianity has existed for centuries. Their faith has not passed through the filter of the Enlightenment and their Christ is not associated with imperial or colonial power and privilege, with the result that they are able to recognize the truly radical nature of the gospel. What is more, from the so-called margins of a globalized world, they are able to discern the extent to which Western Christianity has been shaped, and often compromised, by its relationship with a culture that underpins and justifies the political and economic interests of powerful and dominant nations. Such discernment leads them to ask uncomfortable questions. For example, in the immediate aftermath of the invasion of Iraq, Vinoth Ramachandra from Sri Lanka observed that the double standards of Western governments in relation to human rights, free trade, weapons of mass destruction, and so on, 'have rarely been publicly challenged by Christian leaders, least of all by missionaries and mission agencies that claim to have a global vision' (Ramachandra, 2003, 4).

Such insights, which imply that syncretism is not something that happens only to other people somewhere else in the world, but that we ourselves may be compromised and in need of deep repentance and renewal, may be very unwelcome. Faced with such a challenge we may be tempted to close our ears and minds to such voices, and even to dismiss them as coming from people whose credibility is not recognized by 'our companions'. To do so would be to repeat the folly of the disciples on the Emmaus road and, like them, cut ourselves off from witnesses of Christ whose testimonies have the power to revive our hope, renew our lives, and lead us towards the restoration of our credibility before a watching world.

Christ incognito

We began this chapter at the point at which the unknown Christ came up beside the two disciples on the road. It is worth recalling that throughout the ensuing conversation he remains unrecognized. The moment of recognition, the epiphany, is still to come. Once that revelation has been given then the disciples recall how their hearts had burned within them during the conversation on the road. But this is remembered in retrospect; throughout the journey itself Christ remains hidden, unknown, incognito.

This simple fact has important applications for us. It means, for example, that our experiences of being alone, abandoned and without Christ, may not actually correspond to reality. This is in no way to trivialize or diminish the pain of feelings of loss and loneliness, but the fact that Christ is not recognized does not mean that he is absent. Indeed, we might suggest that for the two walkers in our story, Christ was in fact more intimately and wonderfully present than he had ever been before; had they ever previously known such a conversation with Jesus as this one? So then, even in the darkest and most despairing moments of our pilgrimage we are not alone; Christ walks beside us even when we mistake him for a stranger who comes, uninvited, out of nowhere.

But there is also a great challenge here: the risen Christ not only accompanies the despairing walkers, but he is now the *unpredictable Christ*. He cannot be restricted and contained; he comes and goes and in the power of a risen life does his gracious work in human lives in mysterious ways that are often unseen and unrecognized. This suggests that to understand the resurrection merely as a doctrine to be believed is to strip it of its glory; Christ is alive in the world, on the open roads where people travel and discuss their disappointments, doing his revealing, healing work in ways that are surprising and mysterious. We may not set limits on when, or where, or how he makes his presence known; rather, we can expect to be continually surprised by the sudden, unanticipated ways in which he comes alongside humble people who seek for the kingdom while confessing their need of grace and fresh understanding.

I end this chapter with an example. Roger Garaudy was a leading French intellectual and a prominent and important Marxist philosopher. Driven by a passionate longing to see the world transformed and the creation of a just and humane society, he walked his own 'Emmaus road' when struggling to come to terms with the betrayal of Communist ideals in the Soviet Union. Garaudy confessed: 'It is an overwhelming experience when a man who has professed himself an atheist for many years discovers that the Christian inside him has always been there. It is overwhelming to accept the responsibility for such a hope' (Garaudy, 1976, 202). Garaudy had found Christ, or perhaps had been found *by* him, not within the church (about which he continued to have grave doubts) but on the open road as a social activist and a militant philosopher. His experience illustrates what has been said above concerning the unpredictability and freedom of the risen Christ, while his humble honesty concerning his surprising discovery of faith must challenge all of us who walk the modern road to Emmaus:

Throughout my life I have asked myself if I was a Christian. For forty years I have answered no, because the question was framed incorrectly, as if Christian faith were incompatible with life as a militant. I am sure now that they are one and that my faith as a militant would have no foundation without that faith. Now I hesitate to answer yes for entirely different reasons. Such a faith appears to me as such an explosive force that it would be vain to claim it before having verified it in an action that matches its power. Such verification can come only at the end of a life, not in its midst before one has fully achieved one's part in creation.

(Garaudy, 1976, 98)

It is sobering to read these words, both because of the great challenge they so clearly express, and because the author's subsequent biography involved a further conversion, this time to Islam, and his involvement in considerable controversy in France as the result of his rejection of received historical accounts of the Holocaust. We are reminded here that at this stage in our story we are still on the road that leads *towards* Emmaus; the journey towards renewed hope and a fresh vision remains in progress, and only as we persevere in the company of the Stranger can we reach the point at which real transformation takes place. As we shall see in the next chapter, genuine faith cannot be coerced, and people remain free, like Roger Garaudy, to turn aside and pursue a different path. But as we shall also discover, to abandon the road that takes us to Emmaus, to separate ourselves from the One who has begun to kindle a fire within our souls, is to close off the possibility of a discovery, an 'unveiling', which is capable of utterly transforming both ourselves and our world.

Whatever may have been the reasons for Garaudy's departure from the road towards Emmaus, the fact remains that he believed that we live at a crucial moment in human history when, in various ways, millions of people are asking the fundamental questions that had led him towards faith. At such a time Christians must surely welcome all who become fellow-travellers on the way towards Emmaus, even as they look out for the presence of the One who joins the company in mysterious yet transforming ways.

Dispatches from the Emmaus road

③

Name: Tatiana Goricheva

Biographical information: Brilliant Russian scholar and philosopher who grew up and was educated in Leningrad during the Communist era. In the 1960s, when it became possible to obtain existentialist literature in the Soviet Union, she began reading the works of Albert Camus and Jean-Paul Sartre and found their descriptions of human alienation in a world without meaning corresponded with her own experience. Together with many Russian intellectuals under Soviet rule, Goricheva experienced a religious conversion that led her to the Orthodox Church. She was part of a group which founded a seminar in Leningrad for the discussion of fundamental philosophical and religious questions, was active in the feminist movement, and helped set up an underground newspaper. Prior to the Moscow Olympics in 1980 she and many of her colleagues were given the choice of imprisonment or exile; Goricheva chose to move to the West and during this enforced exile she developed a penetrating critique of religion and culture in the context of great material prosperity.

> I was born in a land from which the traditional values of culture, religion and morality had been deliberately and successfully eradicated; I was on a journey from nowhere to nowhere: I had no roots and would go into an empty, meaningless future. In school essays I wrote the sort of thing that was expected, that I loved my country and Lenin and my mother – but all that was a glib lie. From childhood on I hated everything around me: I hated the people with petty cares and anxieties, indeed they disgusted me; I hated my parents ... I seethed with rage when I thought how I had been brought into the world without wanting to be there and in a completely absurd way. I even hated nature with its eternal round and tedious rhythm: summer, autumn, winter ... (Goricheva, 1986, 10–11)

> For us existentialism was the first taste of freedom, the first public discussion that was not forbidden ... Sartre could bring us to the verge of despair at which faith

begins. His central idea, that human beings make a free choice every second, is indeed a Christian notion . . . I much enjoyed being a 'brilliant' student and the pride of the philosophical faculty; I enjoyed cultured conversation with sophisticated intellectuals, stood at the speaker's desk at academic conferences, made ironical comments and when it came to intellectual matters was only satisfied with the best. However, in the evenings I kept company with outsiders and people from the lowest levels of society – thieves, psychological cases and drug addicts. We got drunk in cellars and attics. Sometimes we broke into a house just for the fun of drinking a cup of coffee and then vanishing again. (1986, 13–15)

Yoga merely opened up the world of the absolute to me, let my spiritual eye perceive a new vertical dimension of being and destroyed my intellectual arrogance . . . it became like a small bridge between the empirical world and the transcendent world. I was doing my Yoga exercise with the mantras wearily and without pleasure . . . But in a Yoga book a Christian prayer, the 'Our Father', was suggested as an exercise . . . I began to say it as a mantra, automatically and without expression. I said it about six times, and then I was suddenly turned inside out. I understood – not with my ridiculous understanding, but with my whole being – that he exists. He, the living, personal God, who loves me and all creatures, who has created the world, who became a human being out of love, the crucified and risen God.

At that moment I understood and grasped the 'mystery' of Christianity, the new, true life. That was real, genuine deliverance. At this moment everything in me changed. The old me died. I gave up not only my earlier values and ideals, but also my old habits.

Finally my heart was also opened. I began to love people. I could understand their suffering and also their lofty destiny, that they are made in the image of God. Immediately after my conversion everyone simply seemed to me to be a miraculous inhabitant of heaven, and I could not wait to do good and to serve human beings and God. (1986, 16–18)

When Christ preached, to reach the souls of men and women he had to transform the experience of fishermen. To penetrate the soul of modern people he has to melt a whole iceberg of impressions; he has to overcome history, education, politics, the trivialization of life, the collapse of morality, aestheticism, the revolution – think of all the things that humanity has piled up over these two thousand years! And it is necessary to return to the clear and sublime commandments for blessedness: 'Blessed are the pure in heart, for they shall see God'. (1986, 38)

A week before the beginning of the Olympic games in Moscow we were given a choice: imprisonment or emigration. We chose the West . . . I had arrived in Vienna. What did I feel? Was it a feeling of freedom? No! I was also free in Russia. Freedom is a gift of God . . . I had the feeling that I had come into a world of forms. Everything in this world found expression, every sense had excellent packaging. Everything here sought to please, was in a hurry to serve people in some way. (1986, 87–8)

I saw my first religious broadcast on television. I thank God that we have atheism and no religious education. What this man said on the screen was more likely to drive more people out of the church than all the clumsy chatter of our paid atheists. Dressed up in a posh way, the self-satisfied preacher had to talk of love. But . . . [he] was a boring bad actor with mechanical and studied gestures. He was faceless. For the first time I understood how dangerous it is to talk about God. Each word must be a sacrifice – filled to the brim with authenticity. Otherwise it is better to keep silent. (1986, 90–1)

I'm now trying to love the well-to-do and self-satisfied church, which is in all things opposed to what proves to be the original idea of the church . . . Difficult times have dawned for the church in the West, more difficult than for the church in the East.

Eureka! I have the solution. Not those who have seen but those who believe are more blessed than those who have seen and then believe. So even the authentic Christians in the West must be more blessed than those of us who have come to faith in Russia. There, like Thomas, we have seen his wounds and touched concretely and visibly his now immortal body. We felt God, and we understood that He is more real than all the world around us.

But here I meet hardly anyone with a comparable experience. And nevertheless I have met true believers. (1986, 96–7)

4

Epiphany!

—◆—

Our story moves towards its climax as, with the sun disappearing beyond the horizon to the West, the walkers approach their destination at Emmaus. Now comes a surprise: the stranger who had joined the fleeing disciples uninvited now proposes to leave them, 'as if he were going further'. However, whereas his initial appearance alongside them on the road was unwelcome and deeply unsettling, the absorbing conversation that has taken place as they have walked together has clearly transformed the attitude of the two companions to such an extent that they now find the prospect of his departure intolerable. This I take to be the explanation of the fact that they now 'urged him strongly' to accept their hospitality and remain with them overnight. To be sure, the reason stated for this invitation is that 'the day is almost over' and to travel alone in the gathering gloom would be an act of madness. Elsewhere Luke has recorded a story told by Jesus in which the extreme dangers of travelling alone on the roads of ancient Palestine outside certain times of the day is vividly illustrated (14.30).

Nonetheless, what really drives this urgent invitation is revealed, I suggest, in the phrase 'Stay with us'. It is the companionship, the *presence* of this still mysterious person that they crave. The offer of hospitality holds the promise of further conversation and, having caught just a glimpse of the possibilities of a transformed worldview, they are unwilling to allow their companion to pass on into the night.

There are lessons for us here. First, there are times of unique opportunity, days, moments even, when we are presented with choices that have the potential to bring dramatic change into our lives. As in this story, such windows of opportunity may open to us in wholly unexpected ways and at times when it has seemed that all hope was gone. Suddenly, and with growing conviction, we become aware of possibilities in life that simply transcend anything we have previously imagined. At this stage, as with the Emmaus two, we may be unable to understand or articulate what it is that is happening to us, but we are conscious of a mysterious birthing of hope deep within us and a growing conviction that the road we have been treading may not be a cul-de-sac after all.

Such fresh insight is not without cost since it brings with it the implication that our existing view of life, which we may have firmly believed to be adequate, perhaps even completely non-negotiable, is in fact rather narrow and confining. What until this moment has seemed to be a 'common sense' view of life in the world now starts to look as though it has actually prevented us from grasping aspects of reality that are capable of enriching human life. And this is scary because it may lead us to break ranks with 'our companions' who, so far as we can tell, remain locked into the worldview we have, until now, shared with them. When the Emmaus walkers urge their new friend, 'Stay with us', this is a decision for change; to invite him into the house involves an intellectual and spiritual openness which has the potential to result in truly revolutionary transformation.

The Danish philosopher Søren Kierkegaard understood well the crucial importance of the kind of experiences we have been describing. His writings published between 1847 and 1855 were interspersed with a series of remarkable prayers which came to the attention of a wider public when they were set to music by the American composer Samuel Barber. Here is one of these prayers:

> Father in Heaven,
> well we know that it is Thou
> that giveth both to will and to do,

that also longing,
when it leads us to renew
the fellowship with our Saviour and
Redeemer,
is from Thee.
Father in Heaven, longing is Thy gift
but when longing lays hold of us,
oh, grant that we might lay hold of the longing!
when it would carry us away,
that we also might give ourselves up!
when Thou art near to summon us,
that we also in prayer might stay near Thee!
When Thou in the longing
dost offer us the highest good,
oh, that we might hold it fast![1]

Kierkegaard's understanding of the mysterious interplay between grace and freedom brings us to the second lesson we must draw from the action of Jesus on arriving in Emmaus. When Luke records that Christ 'acted as if he were going further', he underscores a fundamental principle concerning the manner in which genuine faith and hope are communicated. In Kierkegaard's terminology, the moment of *longing* is given as a gift, but it may be spurned and then lost. The longing has to be taken hold of, held fast. Real faith is not something conventional and self-evident, even less can it be imposed or retained by force. Christ might have blinded his companions with a blaze of resurrection glory that would have had them falling in the dust at his feet, but instead he respects their freedom, offering them opportunity for the radical reorientation of their lives and the recovery of hope.

What this means is that embedded at the very centre of the Christian story is the principle that *genuine faith cannot be compelled.* Earlier in this book we have been reminded that when Christianity became the dominant religion in Europe, attaining both social prestige and political power, it quickly forgot the example of its Founder and invented a whole battery of methods to coerce people into allegiance to this religion, and then to ensure that they never abandoned it. The Christ of the Emmaus road, who elsewhere in Luke's Gospel is said to have depicted God himself in a revolutionary manner as 'the waiting Father' (15.20), largely faded from Christian memory, despite the constant celebration of rituals involving bread and wine which, it can be argued, contain distinct echoes of this very narrative. This loss of memory and the substitution of the stern, demanding God who imposes belief as a matter of law and custom, sowed the seeds of secularity across the continent, eventually provoking a revolt in which people began to march under different banners in the quest for human freedom.

In Eastern Europe this secular quest for human liberation took a form in the twentieth century that resulted in the dramatic removal of all the inherited social status and privileges enjoyed by institutional Christianity throughout earlier centuries. However, the Czech theologian Jan Milic Lochman observes that, once the shock of this new context had been absorbed, it came to be recognized as a positive opportunity to rediscover the true source and nature of Christian identity in the world. With all the props and social supports of Christendom removed, believers realized that the gospel itself contained an imperative demanding the rejection once and for all of 'the *obligatory, compulsory God* whom believers impose on their fellow human beings, over-riding their minds and consciences and even threatening sanctions in the case of non-conformity'. The repudiation of *this* God, Lochman says, was demanded not simply by the social and historical circumstances in which Christians found themselves, but above all, 'because we are led to do so by fresh reflection on the source of our faith (Lochman, 1988, 44). This is now precisely the lesson that Christians in Western Europe and North America must learn, recognizing their Emmaus road situation as a gracious opportunity to encounter the God who, while absolutely not at our beck and call, still waits to be invited to remain with those whose hearts he sets on fire.

Freedom, secularity and pluralism

In an era of growing and seemingly irreversible religious pluralism, we must ask whether the principle discussed above has relevance beyond the experience of contemporary Christians and might have application in the lives of those identified earlier in this study as likely companions on the modern road to Emmaus. Discussions concerning secularity, freedom of belief, and the role of law in enforcing and maintaining conformity to what is understood to be holy and just, take place constantly within Islam. Indeed, for vast numbers of Muslims now living in modern, secular societies, such debates are characterized by great passion and intensity since they concern issues that go to the very heart of Muslim self-understanding and identity. As Kenneth Cragg has put it in a brief but brilliant essay, while the politicization of Christianity can be seen as a departure from the original vision of this faith, the case with Islam is quite different since, from a very early stage, it developed 'an amalgam of faith and power so strong that apostasy from the one was treason to the other'. Islam thus became 'the most political of all the great religions' (Cragg, 1998, 16–17).

Nonetheless, as we have previously noted, Islam is not an unchanging monolith and questions concerning the nature of religious experience, and the ways in which love for, and obedience to, God may best be promoted can draw quite different answers. Critical reflection on the past, on the actual experience of the alliance of faith and power under Muslim rule, combine with new questions posed by the present, with its challenge to work out ways of practising the faith in the context of resolutely secular societies, to stimulate fresh debate and a search for new answers. As Cragg says, the strength of Islamic theism means that Muslims are unlikely ever to concede to arguments emanating from 'secular philosophies or Western pressures' (nor should they). But the case for religious liberty, including the renunciation of coercion in matters of faith, and an active and genuine engagement in dialogue, 'can be rightly and effectively made from within' this religion. As he notes, the Shahadah confesses Muhammad as Rasul-Allah, 'the messenger' – not the generalissimo – of Allah (1998, 54–5).

What then of our humanist companions on the journey? Does the discussion above suggest that religious people are about simply to concede the fundamental correctness of the Western Enlightenment tradition, allowing the 'public square' to remain empty, while they withdraw to the sphere of private life, leaving politics and economics untroubled by critical questions arising from prophetic faith? Of course not. Such an outcome is precisely one that many political leaders appear to want, with religions reduced to being docile supporters of a thoroughly secular status quo. Power can then be exercised without being called to account and 'faith' is used to underwrite a world system that produces and sustains quite grotesque inequalities and injustices. I propose, to the contrary, that while a faith renewed through the rediscovery of its own transcendent source and the recognition of its proper calling in the world will affirm the legitimate independence and freedom of politics, it will challenge secularism as a worldview and suggest to humanist fellow-travellers on the road that our forgetfulness of God has resulted in a situation in which, despite our best intentions, we are creating societies that prevent human flourishing.

In actual fact, as we have noted previously, there are growing indications that humanism is becoming increasingly self-critical, chastened by a historical record that clearly confirms Madeleine Bunting's observation that violence and despotism 'are not monopolies of the religious' and that most of the worst terrors of the twentieth century were the products of atheist regimes. Bunting argues powerfully that 'our future as a species is too precarious' to allow the wisdom of religious traditions to be ignored and she calls for 'vastly more humility and more sustained curiosity about how previous ages and other cultures have understood the nature of the human person and our yearning for freedom' (Bunting, 2006).[2]

Here then, at the end of our walk to Emmaus, we stand together, chastened, still puzzled, yet with a mysterious sense that change is under way and that we may be on the edge of something genuinely new. Our narrative describes how, at the passionate urging of his companions, the unknown stranger 'went in to stay with them'. It's time to go inside.

The moment of recognition

The story now moves swiftly towards its climax. Secondary descriptive details are stripped away and we are invited to witness the scene as the travellers take supper together. We are immediately made aware of a significant shift in the nature of the relationship between the Emmaus two and their guest as he now takes centre stage: 'When he was at the table with them, he took bread, gave thanks, broke it and began to give it to them.' The guest has become the host; those offering hospitality find themselves on the receiving end of the gift of grace; the seekers are surprisingly transformed into the sought! Something in the action of the stranger at this climactic point brings about a sudden, life-transforming moment of recognition: 'Then their eyes were opened and they recognised him'.

As we noted at the beginning of this book, this sudden flash of revelation, and the equally dramatic statement that in the same instant 'he disappeared from their sight', has made this scene irresistible to a succession of great artists. Caravaggio painted it twice; his 1601 depiction, now in the National Gallery in London, is found on the cover of this volume. This extraordinary painting wonderfully portrays the utter astonishment of the two disciples. One begins to rise from his chair (we almost hear the scraping of the wooden legs on the floor), while the other involuntarily throws his arms wide open, creating an enormous depth to the picture and almost seeming to thrust his left hand through the surface of the canvas. Between them, and at the central point, is a surprisingly original representation of Jesus, shorn of traditional Catholic symbols of divinity, and reminding us of the youthfulness of the Christ who was later to be described by the hymn-writer Isaac Watts as 'the young prince of glory'. On the edge of the table nearest to the viewer the artist has painted a basket of fruit that appears to be in imminent danger of falling to the floor, a device that draws us into the picture, inviting us to share this epiphany.

Equally remarkable, although quite different in style and content, is the 1628 painting by Rembrandt, *Christ at Emmaus*, now in Paris (see the frontispiece). Rembrandt is the supreme painter of the stories of the Bible, and the narrative of the Emmaus walk repeatedly attracted his attention. However, this picture, aptly described by Simon Schama as 'an essay in sacred stupefaction', is unique; it matches and even surpasses Caravaggio in its portrayal of the awe-fulness of the moment of recognition for the disciples, but it goes beyond this in capturing the sense of mystery, of what may truly be called the 'holy' in this scene.[3] As to the disciples, only one of them is visible to us, a staggering picture of a man whose world has just imploded in the light of the risen Christ, at whom he stares with eyes standing out from his head. His companion has disappeared, his head buried on the lap of Christ before whom he kneels, his hair just visible against the background of the cloth on the table, literally standing on end.

In the background we glimpse what appears to be the figure of a woman, presumably involved in domestic activity related to the delivery of the supper. What this figure does, however, is to increase the element of mystery, of ambiguity in this painting; we are witnesses of a real event here, and yet something is taking place that is uncanny, unique, something that *transcends* normal reality. The figure of Christ is real; this is the man who has accompanied the disciples on the road and engaged with them in rational (if profoundly disturbing) conversation. But such is the genius of the artist that we sense that this figure, so clearly depicted here, as in Rembrandt's wonderful nativity scenes, as the light of the world, is about to vanish. Epiphanies are by definition *moments* of revelation; they do not last and, while stimulating faith, they do not remove the need to continue *living by faith*.

This brings us to the question of exactly what it was in the actions and words of Jesus in the house at Emmaus that triggered the disciples' realization of the identity of the stranger. Scholars have pointed out that the language used here concerning the breaking of bread corresponds almost exactly with the words found on the lips of Jesus at the Last Supper (22.19). However, the Emmaus two were not present on that occasion, but they may well have been among the much larger group of Christ's followers who, at an earlier stage in his ministry, had witnessed him take five loaves and two fishes and, having given thanks and broken the bread, gave food to the disciples 'to set before the people' (9.16). Did they now recall that stunning event which had played such a key role in creating the hope among his followers that he might be the one who was going to redeem Israel? And if so, do they now begin to see the ghastly events of the past few days in an altogether different light, one that illuminates the stranger's previously incomprehensible claim that the Messiah had to 'suffer these things and then enter into his glory'?

At this point we need to pick up the fundamental question left unanswered earlier in this book: why did Jesus *have* to suffer and die? In particular, why did he have to experience the ignominy and humiliation of death by crucifixion, a form of execution specifically designed by the Romans to brand its victims as enemies of the state? Richard Horsley and Neil Asher Silberman describe Roman crucifixion as an 'oppressive, genocidal, imperial mode of torture', and they continue:

> The stench, screams and horrible sights of public places of execution on the outskirts of every Roman city offered a grotesque counter-image to the elegance and architectural splendor of the temples, forums and plazas within. The cross and the Corinthian column were two sides of the Roman experience. One offered shade and shelter to all those who would accept the Roman world's logic and structures of power; the other systematically transformed anyone branded as an enemy of the Roman order from

a living, breathing person into a bruised, bloated, almost unrecognisable corpse.

(Horsley and Silberman, 1997, 86)

It is worth recalling here that when Luke describes the events that led up to the death of Christ there are unmistakable references to the political dimension of the charges made against him. He is accused of 'subverting our nation' and opposing the 'payment of taxes to Caesar' (23.2). Later, Jesus is said to have fomented trouble 'all over Judea' and now to pose a threat to civil order at the very centre of power (23.5). Of course, the charges made against Christ were perverse in that they implied that he was guilty of the usual forms of insurrection, depicting him as simply the latest in a long line of political revolutionaries. But this should not lead us to ignore the fact that the sheer goodness of Jesus, his endless compassion for the suffering and the oppressed, and his bold and courageous declaration of the ethical demands of Israel's God, were indeed subversive of a society built on greed and structured in the interests of the privileged and powerful. As Horsley and Silberman point out, there were alternative forms of execution in the ancient world, including beheading or stoning to death, and the fact that Christ was crucified is eloquent testimony 'to the depth and the clarity of the threat that he posed' (1997, 86).

How else shall we explain the fact that when the Roman governor Pilate offered to set free either Jesus or Barabbas (who is said to have led 'an insurrection in the city', and to have been a murderer, 23.19), the religious and political leaders of the nation chose the violent revolutionary, shouting in chorus for the release of a terrorist whose threat they understood and could cope with. By contrast, the challenge posed by the Rabbi from Nazareth was of an altogether different kind and, as his following grew and a revolution of love and justice began to spread, this was a threat to 'normal politics' that was simply too great to tolerate.

On the road to Emmaus Jesus had pointed out to his broken and despairing disciples that the experience of the crucified Messiah was absolutely consistent with the message and the biographies of the prophets who had preceded him. Their invariable experience had been of rejection and suffering; as a later Christian writer was to say, true prophets were tortured, flogged and imprisoned, during their lives they were 'destitute, persecuted and mistreated – the world was not worthy of them' (Hebrews 11.36–38). And these same prophets, anticipating the coming of One who would represent the culmination and fulfilment of the tradition to which they belonged, recognized that his victory over evil, and the bringing into history of a different order of things, would inevitably involve rejection, suffering and death: Christ had to 'suffer these things and then enter his glory'.

Of course, the question concerning the meaning of the death of Christ can be – must be – answered at different levels. It is the witness of the New Testament, for example, that the judicial murder of Jesus of Nazareth, whose life would later be summed up in the simple phrase, he 'went around doing good' (Acts 10.38), demanded the recognition that deep forces of evil were at work in this drama. Seen in this light there is a *cosmic* dimension to the Cross that relates it to forms of wickedness that appear to be embedded in mysterious ways within the very structures of human societies and cultures. Such language once seemed archaic and redundant to modern people who imagined themselves freed from 'mere superstition', but the dark and long shadows cast by the horrors of man's unending 'inhumanity to man' have resulted in a situation in which it no longer seems strange to describe certain acts as 'demonic'.[4] Indeed, for many contemporary people the journey towards Emmaus has been triggered by terrifying encounters with depths of wickedness that we had naively thought consigned to history. Precisely at this point, the epiphany at Emmaus shines the light of hope into our world, bringing the astonishing realization that what had seemed an utter tragedy is in fact the means of the defeat and overthrow of the dark and destructive powers at work in the world. Those powers now stand exposed and judged, their hold on human lives broken, as the divine vindication of Jesus becomes the beginning of true human liberation.

Mention of 'divine vindication' points us towards another level of explanation of the Messiah's death, that which relates it to the action of God himself. Later in Luke's narrative Christ again appears to his disciples and makes it clear that news of his death and rising is to be shared with 'all nations' so that they may come to 'repentance and forgiveness of sins' (24.47). That is to say, the message of the Cross is not a private concern, confined within a religious cult from which the majority of humankind are excluded. Paul can later claim that 'God was reconciling the world to himself in Christ' (2 Corinthians 5.19), while another follower of Jesus, reminding fellow-believers that the sacrifice made on Calvary has brought the forgiveness of their sins, immediately adds, 'and not only ours but also the sins of the whole world' (1 John 2.2). We may well wonder how the universal dimensions of the hope of the gospel, the joyful announcement that, through the Cross of Christ, God has made provision for the healing of the sickness of the world, have so often suffered eclipse within the church. Why have Christians repeatedly reduced and narrowed the horizons of this hope, claiming what belongs to the whole world as if it were their private possession?

Whatever the answer to these questions, the fact remains that the revolutionary message of the crucified Messiah cannot be suppressed or contained. As literary critic Jack Miles puts it in the brilliant opening to his book, *Christ: A Crisis in the Life of God*:

> All mankind is forgiven, but the Lord must die. This is the revolutionary import of the epilogue that, two thousand years ago, a group of radical Jews appended to the sacred scripture of their religion. Because they did so, millions in the West today worship before the image of a deity executed as a criminal, and – no less important – other millions who never worship at all carry within their cultural DNA a religiously derived suspicion that

somehow, someday, 'the last will be first and the first last' (Matthew 20.16).

(Miles, 2001, 3)[5]

In discussing the impact of the story of the crucifixion of Jesus on the Western conscience, Miles argues that it has resulted in an almost subliminal conviction, lodged 'deep in the political consciousness of the West', that 'the apparent loser may be the real winner unrecognized'. He suggests that it is because of this that 'in the West no regime can declare itself above review. All power is conditional; and when the powerless rise, God may be with them' (2001, 3).

It becomes clear that the eye-popping, mind-blowing epiphany at Emmaus, together with the other reported appearances of the risen Christ at this time, are far from being innocuous, apolitical tales. Evidence for this claim is to be found in the manner in which these narratives shaped the character of the earliest Christian movement so that the life, death and resurrection of Jesus provided a model for human life that was radically counter-cultural in the context of a world increasingly dominated by the Roman empire. The same writer we have noticed insisting that the death of Jesus provided forgiveness 'for the sins of the whole world', immediately goes on to remind those who have recognized this fact that they 'must walk as Jesus did' (1 John 2.6). The letters of Paul, so profoundly influential within the emerging Christian movement in the great urban centres of the ancient world, have been described as containing 'a frontal assault on the empire', providing the followers of the crucified Messiah with the resources to 'reimagine the world as if Christ, not the powers, were sovereign' (Walsh and Keesmaat, 2004, 84). Perhaps most striking of all is the fact that the New Testament ends with an extraordinary work that explicitly summons Christians to withstand the seductive power of Roman propaganda and, even at the cost of their lives, to remain faithful to the Christ whom they confessed as the true saviour of the world. Richard Bauckham describes the book of Revelation as a 'thorough-going prophetic critique of the system of Roman power' and 'the most powerful piece of political resistance literature from the period of the early Empire'. He adds that the author of this book understood very clearly that the confession of Christ's Lordship led to an inevitable clash with 'Rome's divine pretensions' (Bauckham, 1993, 38).

The death of death

If the astonishment of the Emmaus two is due to the transformation that the epiphany brings to their understanding of the life and death of Jesus, it also obviously results from the fact that they are now witnesses of his return to life. It is a disturbing thing to, quite literally, encounter a 'dead man walking'!

At this point it might be assumed that the dialogue between Christians and some of their companions on the modern road to Emmaus will come to a juddering halt. After all, belief in the resurrection of Jesus is a matter of *faith* and in a modern, scientific culture an event of this kind simply cannot happen. However, before we reach such a conclusion we need to recognize that there may be more common ground here than is often granted. The darkest shadows creating despair and hopelessness for the original travellers as they left Jerusalem, were cast by *death*. They walked together through what the Bible famously calls 'the valley of the shadow of death', but were unable to affirm with the psalmist, 'I will fear no evil.' God had gone missing on the road to Emmaus, with the result that death appeared absolutely triumphant and now cast ever deeper shadows of futility and meaninglessness over human life and achievement.

Compare that context with the sober verdict of contemporary humanist scholars who, reflecting on the underlying forces that drive culture, conclude that a central discovery of modern thought is that 'of all the things that move man, one of the principal ones is his terror of death' (Becker, 1973, 11). In earlier times death could be faced with courage because belief in immortality drew its sting and gave purpose and hope to human existence in this world, but since the Renaissance we have increasingly found ourselves on a path without such hope. As a result modern people are driven to construct ideologies and projects capable of suppressing their deepest anxieties and providing some assurance that human existence remains meaningful. But the projects always fail; death remains as the ultimate reality, and we too find ourselves in the 'valley of the shadow of death' with no comforting presence to remove our fears. As Zygmunt Bauman puts it:

> We have come to see as 'progress' the relentless 'emancipation' of man from 'constraints'. We have learnt (and have been taught) to view the primal human bonds ... as oppression. Throughout the modern era political legislators, warriors of free trade and philosophers joined forces in order to free man from that oppression. Bonds were now to be freely chosen, freely entered into and abandoned ... Bonds were now to pass the test of happiness; or, rather, of the promise of happiness they carry. Most certainly, this was liberation from the many petty slaveries of life. But the liberated have been ushered into new, no less awesome slavery. Life now had little else to define itself by as the movement toward death. With everything that fills it with contents reduced to ephemerality ... it turns into a long dress rehearsal of non-being.
> (Bauman, 1992, 49)[6]

It is possible to react to this kind of analysis of the human condition with a stoical acceptance of the inevitability of the tragic nature of the world. Indeed, it may be surprising to discover that just such a response can be found within the Bible: the writer of Ecclesiastes concludes that since human destiny is to rot in the earth and be forgotten ('There is no remembrance of men of old, and even those yet to come will not be remembered by those who follow', 1.11), human life must be judged 'utterly meaningless' (1.2). The remedy for despair when confronted with such a view of reality is simply to resolve to go on living; the world may be, as Camus saw so clearly, 'absurd', but genuinely humanistic values can survive this discovery and sustain people in lives that are truly good and life-enhancing.

That such a reaction to the threat to meaning posed by death is possible is demonstrated by countless examples of humanists who have indeed lived exemplary lives, full of compassion and mercy and tirelessly committed to justice and equality in this world. However, the question must be asked whether this kind of 'heroic dedication' can survive in a historical and cultural context in which the spiritual resources for such a life have all but withered and died. As Ernest Becker observed more than thirty years ago, the one-dimensionality of late modern culture has unleashed upon the world an ideology of commercialism unprecedented in human history, resulting in a situation in which modern man 'is drinking and drugging himself out of awareness, or he spends his time shopping, which is the same thing' (Becker, 1973, 284).

The questions being raised here are not abstract and theoretical but have a direct bearing on the future of humankind and the planet we inhabit together. Indeed, contemporary concerns about ecological devastation, right and good though they are, too often fail to get to the underlying causes of the destructive ways of life that threaten to destroy the earth and all its life forms. No mere modification of our existing worldview and the manner of human life that results from it can save us; what is required is a critical evaluation of the very foundations of modern culture and a new openness and honesty concerning the repressed fears that fuel beliefs and actions that are driving us to the edge of catastrophe. In other words, our Emmaus dialogue is more needed now than ever and offers hope that another way ahead might be found for the human family in which death is no longer denied, suppressed or trivialized. Such a path must go via the house at Emmaus where two despairing people looked into the face of the risen Jesus and bore testimony to the fact that they had been witnesses of the death of death. In the light of that event Ernest Becker's words take on a profound significance: 'Who knows what form the forward momentum of life will take in the time ahead or what use it will make of our anguished searching' (1973, 285).[7]

The burning heart

The moment of revelation in the house at Emmaus in which 'their eyes were opened and they recognised him', is immediately followed by the disappearance of the risen Christ, so that the epiphany becomes the foundation for a life of faith. We might say that the normal experience of human existence in this world is resumed, but it is a 'normality' transformed by an encounter that has broken apart the limits of the disciples' previous understanding of reality. To use an eastern term, these are people who have discovered the 'really real' and now recognize that their previous view of the world was distressingly one-dimensional. It is as though a film of their lives, shot up to this point in black and white, has suddenly been flooded with colour and a landscape that had always been familiar now appears a totally different place.

However, notice that when the Emmaus two find themselves alone, their conversation turns back to what had happened during the walk from Jerusalem: 'Were not our hearts burning within us while he talked with us on the road and opened the Scriptures to us?' The reference to 'burning hearts' forms a contrast with their unknown companion's rebuke that they had been 'slow of heart' to believe the revelation granted to Israel's prophets. In other words, during the journey to Emmaus an unseen, inward transformation was already under way, triggered by a fresh understanding of the meaning of those Scriptures with which the disciples were so familiar. To use the language of the Old Testament scholar Walter Brueggemann, prophetic texts that had 'lingered' across the centuries, revered, lovingly preserved and constantly read, had suddenly *exploded* into life. The exposition of these texts by Jesus revealed a depth of meaning and a startling contemporary relevance that his followers had never previously dreamt of.

There is a question here for the modern Church: if the prophetic texts of ancient Israel, originally so powerful and controversial that they provoked the very reactions against these men we have earlier noted, could, over the centuries, become neutered, read and heard within systems of interpretation that rendered them incapable of disturbing the status quo or bringing about social and cultural transformation, might the same thing happen to the literature we know as the New Testament?

- Does the Emmaus story remind us that all human language is subject to change, so that words and phrases that once communicated meaning with dynamic power grow old and weary and cease to be challenging and disturbing?
- Worse still, words that in particular contexts possessed explosive power can become so familiar that they come to function in a manner that makes change impossible.
- Are we here brought face to face with the crisis of modern Christianity, especially in its Protestant form, in that preaching and teaching has become so predictable and boring that the last thing expected by those who continue to subject themselves to it is that their hearts might be warmed!

Nearly fifty years ago, one of the great preachers of the twentieth century observed that most Protestant sermons involved 'the mere grinding out of a routine vocabulary – God, grace, sin, justification – which produces a kind of Christian gobbledegook that never gets under anybody's skin and at most elicits the reaction: "Well, that's the way the minister *has* to speak, but what's it to me?"' (Thielicke, 1965, 2–3). However, perhaps the modern Emmaus road, the place where death appears to reign unchallenged and life is reduced to creating strategies designed to avoid confronting reality, is precisely the context within which ancient texts and seemingly redundant narratives are likely to explode into life. Might it not be that, now as then, the voice of prophecy will be heard afresh, rising above the babble of *Big Brother* and *The Weakest Link*, renewing genuine hope for weary travellers who discover their hearts 'strangely warmed'?

Much as such an outcome is to be devoutly hoped for, notice finally that it will demand the hard work and utter dedication of a new generation of prophetic teachers gifted with what Brueggemann calls 'a capacity for imagination and intuition, coupled with courage' and a determination to demonstrate how these ancient texts may be 'concretely relocated and specifically readdressed as illuminating and revelatory in contemporary contexts' (Brueggemann, 2000, 18).

Dispatches from the Emmaus road

Name: Edith Black

Biographical information: A brilliant American academic with a great gift for languages, Edith Black was a recognized expert in cuneiform studies at University College at Berkeley, California. In the 1960s she became involved in radical politics but eventually suffered a breakdown that led to a deep personal crisis. The text below is taken from an article with the title 'A rediscovery of the Christian Faith', and describes a pilgrimage that has all the hallmarks of the 'Emmaus walk' that we have discussed in this book.

When I was at Union Theological Seminary I encountered God in the liberation movements of which I was a participant – in the civil rights, anti-war and student movements and in woman's liberation. The God of the biblical faith was for me the one who heard the cries of the oppressed and delivered them. I saw the dialectic of judgement and grace being worked out in the midst of social upheaval. I steeped myself in the prophets and developed, by exhaustive reading of Marxist theory, a sharply analytical, prophetic critique of American capitalism. But for me in those exciting, march-filled days God was always out there, fighting an oppressor who was out there, an oppressor in the evil structure of society, the principalities and powers. I had little understanding of the oppressor inside the deepest part of each of us.

My deep involvement in the movement enriched me tremendously and in no way do I look back on it with regret. But like so many other dedicated radicals, I quickly burned out . . . I initially dropped out because my health broke down, but it wasn't this that kept me out, for had I known a loving, empathetic response to being sick on the part of my movement friends I would have regained strength to come back fighting. But that is exactly what I did not experience. I was sick and few visited me, hardly anyone from my family, my academic and movement friends . . . If it wasn't for the love of a husband who stood by me and provided for me, a husband who learned how to love growing up in a missionary family, I think I would have gone stark raving mad.

I eventually regained my health and resumed studies at University College, Berkeley, California ... I hoped to restore my lost sense of self-confidence by pursuing an academic subject in which I had always excelled, the study of ancient languages ... But after two years of constant study it was clear that the academic game was all too much like the games I had encountered elsewhere ... I only ended up more disillusioned and embittered, lost in a morass of self-pity. The biblical tradition meant little to me any more, for I had despaired of any meaning in life.

It was in my darkest hour, in the moment of deepest despair, that faith began to well up in me like a bubbling spring. In the midst of my greatest awareness of the tragedy of the human condition, the inevitability of human sin, I began, miraculously, to hope ... I realized now that I had laid expectations on others that only a transcendent God could fulfill. I saw clearly for the first time that the gospel message is the final solution to the human dilemma, the only real answer to the agonizing question: why is truth so often on the scaffold and wrong so often on the throne? In Christ I saw embodied the suffering love which does not succeed on worldly terms (cross) but is nonetheless victorious (resurrection), the paradox which is beyond all human understanding.

What I experienced in the 'hour I first believed' can only be described as 'amazing grace', as a mighty onrush of love, as God's unconditional acceptance ... Coming to know Christ can be likened to culture shock when the old ego-props are knocked down and the rug literally pulled out from under one's feet. A maturing relationship with God involves the pain of continual self-confrontation as well as the joy of self-fulfillment, a continual dying and rising again, a continual rebirth, the dialectic of judgement and grace. For the first time in my life I have begun to have the strength to face myself as I am, without excuse but equally important, without guilt. I know that I am sinful but I could not bear this knowledge if I did not also know that I am accepted.

One of the weaknesses of Marxist thinking is that love is not central to it. I have always treasured Che Guevara's words: 'At the risk of seeming ridiculous, let me say that a true revolutionary must be guided by great feelings of love'. But why is it that he almost had to apologize? 'He who does not know love does not know God, for God is love.' That sums it all up for me. Loving care for each other, real sensitivity to each other's needs is the mark of true Christians, not right doctrines, right ritual etc. etc.

I know now that the struggle to humanize the world, the revolution, is a continual process without final resolution until that day when God acts decisively to pull it all together. But as a Christian I can participate in that struggle without succumbing either to despair or to a false optimism . . . I know that I will always be one of Jesus' zealot disciples, with the disciples' question at the ascension forever on my lips: 'Now Lord will you finally deliver power to the people?' I will always walk the delicate tightrope between an idolatrous tendency to absolutize revolution and a pietistic copout. But it is on that kind of razor's edge that a Christian must always stand, living in the tension of being 'in the world but not of it'. (Black, 1973, 18–20)

5

Return to the city

In the previous chapter we reached the climax of the biblical narrative that has provided the framework for this book. There is a final scene that we have still to describe and discuss, but before doing this I want to pause and reflect on the implications of the epiphany at Emmaus with regard to the contemporary context to which I have attempted to relate this story at various points in the preceding pages.

I have suggested that the condition of the disciples on the road to Emmaus, involving the loss of previous certainties and the erosion of hope, corresponds in significant ways to the historical and cultural context within which many people in the modern world – Christians, adherents of other faiths, and ethical humanists – find themselves. But of course, Luke's narrative does not leave the disciples in that situation. Even on the road they are, despite their own perceptions to the contrary, *not* abandoned and *not* alone, and when they arrive at their destination their situation is transformed, as we have seen. The truly revolutionary extent of that transformation will become evident later in this chapter. However, if the darkness and despair of the trek away from Jerusalem, along a road from which God seemed to have gone missing, provides a metaphor of our experience in a post-modern and post-Christendom world, the critical question here is whether the epiphany at the conclusion of that journey can also be related to our context in ways that might suggest a basis on which *genuine hope might be recovered*.

As the 'Dispatches from the Emmaus road' at the conclusion of the previous two chapters have movingly illustrated, the story of the crucified and risen Christ has repeatedly become the foundation for hope in the lives of individuals who find their own biographies reflecting the pattern of the journey of those first disciples, so that they too are 'surprised by joy'. It is particularly significant that Tatiana Goricheva describes her pilgrimage as one that involved reaching 'the verge of despair at which faith begins'. That is to suggest that the confusion and spiritual barrenness that characterizes the road to Emmaus is not inimical to genuine faith. On the contrary, it is precisely when the dreams we have trusted are exposed as fantasies that are powerless to deliver what was promised, or worse still, turn into living nightmares, it is then that the search for deeper foundations for life may begin in earnest.

It is not surprising then that across the Western world we witness a renewed quest for transcendence and a growing recognition of the need to discover a secure basis for values that are capable of sustaining meaningful human life and restraining the violence and greed that threatens the whole of creation. As I have suggested earlier, Christians in the modern West find themselves thrust into the gathering darkness of the Emmaus road precisely because, despite the obvious opportunity that this context might seem to offer them as witnesses to Christ, in the eyes of many of those who are disillusioned with the modern world and seek alternative models of human life and community, institutional Christianity appears discredited and obsolete. We recall again Goricheva's searching comments concerning television evangelists who are 'boring, bad actors' and her conclusion that we have no right to speak of God unless every word is 'a sacrifice – filled to the brim with authenticity'.

I suggest then that, although Christians confess that Christ is risen from the dead (and this confession is fundamentally important to the survival of the faith), they too need a fresh epiphany, a renewed sense of the *presence* of the One so confessed, and a transforming vision able to renew hope, reinvigorate faith, and prepare them for what is likely to be

God's surprising (and almost certainly disturbing) future in the twenty-first century. Ernest Becker, whose work has been referred to earlier and represents one of the most significant analyses of modern culture known to me, observed that the 'ideology of modern commercialism has unleashed a life of invidious comparison unprecedented in human history'. Becker believed that institutional Christianity had been sucked into this evil system and shown itself to be powerless before the onslaught of rampant consumerism. However, he distinguished Christianity in its modern, Western form from what he described as the 'primitive' faith of believers and said that if the Church 'took its own message seriously' it was uniquely placed to challenge any 'one-dimensional immortality ideology' and release human beings from the intolerable burden of seeking to create meaning through their achievements in amassing wealth, gaining celebrity, or exercising power over other people (Becker, 1975, 86). We have yet to discover whether Christianity in the modern West will recover a vision capable of equipping it as a credible witness to its crucified and risen Lord in the coming century.

What then of our companions on the Emmaus road? As we have repeatedly observed, critical thought in the humanist tradition provides us with searching analyses of the condition of human societies and cultures. Indeed, there are times when the work of contemporary sociologists is characterized by such depth and seriousness that one is inclined to think that they are the true inheritors of the ancient prophetic traditions working in the world today. Just as an Isaiah or a Jeremiah was dismissed by those holding power and enjoying privilege in ancient Israel, accused of ridiculous overstatement and unwarranted pessimism, so today when boundless confidence is placed in the process of economic globalization, those who insist on pointing out the human consequences of such processes are unlikely to find themselves rewarded with acclaim and honours. Consider, for example, Zygmunt Bauman's extraordinary description of the extent of the crisis that confronts the human race at the beginning of the twenty-first century:

> What threatens the planet now is not just another round
> of self-inflicted damage . . . but a catastrophe to end all
> catastrophes, a catastrophe that would leave no human
> being behind to record it, to ponder it and derive a les-
> son from it, let alone to learn and apply that lesson.
>
> (Bauman, 2006, 72)

This is clearly a clarion call, challenging naive optimism and foolish complacency and summoning all people of good will to action in defence of the world and all its life forms. Christians should be grateful for such companions on the Emmaus journey, even when those fellow-travellers are inclined to point out uncomfortable facts concerning the ways in which religion has become compromised and has served ends in conflict with its own original vision of the world.

But what of *hope* in the context of the crisis so brilliantly and alarmingly described in writings like these? Here the parallel between the prophets of old and the sociologists of today is less obvious, because while the former imagined a different world from the one they saw around them pre-cisely because their hope rested in the God who was deter-mined to 'make all things new', modern thought excludes such transcendent reference points. Thus, although Bauman states that it is 'the task of the living to keep hope alive', the final chapter of his book dealing with modern fears bears the ambiguous title 'Thought Against Fear (or, an inconclusive conclusion for those who may ask what might be done)'. It is difficult not to conclude that the brilliance of the analysis of the global crisis of our times is not matched here by a well-grounded hope for the future.

So then, Christians and humanists are once again found occupying similar ground. Here we may recall Jacques Ellul's words in the 'Dispatch' at the conclusion of Chapter 2, to the effect that human beings have lost hope because God is silent: 'Such is the basic spiritual reality of this age – God is turned away. God is absent. God is silent.' Despite Bauman's inability to offer a secure foundation for hope in the face of the terrors of our age, on the last pages of the book mentioned above he links the task of sociology with that of ancient prophecy and suggests the sociological agenda must give priority to 'redeeming' (his word) older ways of thinking that could offer a foundation for 'a hope that can make – will make, ought to make – the bold act of hoping possible' (Bauman, 2006, 176).

What this seems to suggest is that modern thought has reached an impasse. There is here a call to return to previous, now abandoned and forgotten wisdom, in a search for a basis for hope that transcends the limited, and limiting, confines of the rationalist tradition that closed up our world in a one-dimensional cul-de-sac. The conclusion must be that, even as Christians may see the present time of uncertainty as a positive opportunity for renewal, so humanist thinkers are using similar language and are searching for new ways forward amid the great crises of our times. That must surely suggest to us that, just as the journey away from Jerusalem provides a metaphor that mirrors our distress and confusion, so the epiphany at Emmaus holds the promise of a new, unimaginable development within human history in which real hope is recovered, old conflicts are overcome, and a new world begins to emerge patterned after a vision that brings justice, peace and love among people and restores a sense of wonder and awe to human life on this planet.

Precisely what the consequences of such an epiphany might be can be judged from the discussion below in which we trace the impact of the vision of the risen Christ on the Emmaus two.

Holy madness

Let us return to our narrative for the final time and, as we do so, we discover that it contains one last, surprising twist. With the epiphany over, the two companions rise from the supper table, put on their coats and go out into the darkness of the night: 'They got up and returned at once to Jerusalem.' Despite the fact that the food on the table had been blessed by Jesus, it looks as though they leave supper uneaten, or perhaps take what they can from the table to sustain them on the journey.

Epiphanies have a tendency to stimulate abnormal behaviour. What makes the action of these two people astonishing is that it runs flatly counter to the reasoning they had employed when trying to persuade the stranger to remain with them overnight. Then they had pointed out the dangers of travelling on the road when the day was 'almost over' and, it will be remembered, had urged this as a reason why he should accept their hospitality. *Now* such reasoning does not appear to enter their heads. The decision to go out into the night, when twilight has given way to complete darkness and the hazards on the road are massively increased, seems to have involved the minimum of discussion. It was an instinctive reaction to an experience that has utterly transformed their world and it leads them to disregard the dangers that had previously loomed so large.

We should be warned: when religion ceases to be merely conventional and, resulting from life-transforming encounters that break apart people's existing view of reality, is infused with a passionate sense of missionary responsibility, it produces forms of behaviour that are bound to appear irrational and reckless to normal, well-adjusted people. Those who have 'seen the Lord' come to view themselves and the surrounding world in a completely new light:

- *Values* that previously seemed of paramount importance become relative, replaced by a fresh order of priorities derived from allegiance to a new Lord and Master.
- *Fears* that paralysed action and set limits to the way in which a 'reasonable' life might be lived are relegated to become necessary risks in the pursuit of life-goals that far transcend the aim of merely surviving.
- *Perceptions* of what constitutes 'sanity' are radically revised: the socially constructed consensus that the 'good life' can be described in purely material and economic categories is seen to be a dangerous falsehood and the unchallengeable

axioms of a culture built on such assumptions come to be viewed as ideological justifications for multiple forms of hideous idolatry.

It is not difficult to understand why, viewed from the perspective of society at large, and indeed (more poignantly), in the eyes of close family members unable to comprehend the cause of such radical changes in behaviour, religion of this kind can look like a kind of 'holy madness' and frequently results in accusations of religious mania. This is a particularly sensitive subject at the present time since those who come to believe that the Christ executed as a criminal, accused of 'subverting our nation' (Luke 23.2), is *alive* and at large in the world, may find themselves under suspicion by the powers that be. Faith in the risen Christ is not, as Zygmunt Bauman appears to suggest, a mere 'life strategy' designed to enable individuals to cope with the fear of death, but is a truly radical belief placing the entire 'way of the world' in question.[1] The primal Christian confession that 'Jesus is Lord', implying that his life and teaching have received the ultimate vindication and that the kingdom he inaugurated has been neither cancelled nor postponed, remains unavoidably subversive. The belief that the crucified Messiah has been raised, that the sting of death has been removed, becomes the foundation for a way of life that runs completely counter to societies designed to facilitate the worship of Mammon.

All of this, I suggest, is to be seen in the extraordinary actions of the Emmaus two as they begin their 'crazy' walk through the darkness of an eastern night. Not only are the real, physical dangers on the road ignored, but little prior planning is in evidence in relation to the challenge of gaining access to the city of Jerusalem in the dead of night. Remember that not many hours before this, these people had retreated from the city, slipping through gates where, one assumes, there was every possibility that they might have been apprehended as people posing a grave threat to national security. Now those gates will be locked and barred and anyone approaching in the darkness would be easily spotted and automatically come under suspicion. While we must be careful not to read too much into this narrative, the point to make here is simply this: from the perspective of normal politics and power the actions of these people are absurd and pathetic.

However, things are not always what they seem to be. What if these 'religious crazies' are in fact people who have 'come to their senses'? What if these marginal characters are actually people in possession of a form of knowledge that is literally world-shaking? And what if, therefore, despite all outward appearances to the contrary, these people, motivated by the gift of hope for a new kind of world, pose a threat to Jerusalem – to the world as it now is – far greater than that presented by either violent insurrection from within, or invading armies from without?

The questions being raised here have an urgent relevance for those of us who are companions on the modern Emmaus road. For example, we need to enquire whether the generally accepted criteria by which we judge the sanity and 'wholeness' of human persons are as scientifically neutral and value-free as we imagine them to be. Societies that define themselves as 'civilized' draw clear boundaries with which to determine what constitutes mental and emotional health. When individuals fall on the wrong side of this line they are referred to specialists trained in therapies designed to restore such unfortunates to normality. Meantime, the majority of people continue to operate within the civilized system, devoted to the pursuit of wealth and pleasure and assured by 'opinion formers', modern educators, and the image-makers who dominate the mass media that such goals constitute the only 'good life' available to contemporary people. Moreover, through the process of globalization, this way of understanding human existence in the world is becoming universal, enticing the minority who have access to the system with its promises of happiness, even as it mocks the majority who have no route of escape from poverty.

But what if, both within the heartlands of the 'civilized' world and at its impoverished peripheries, growing numbers of people have been to Emmaus and, having caught sight there of 'another King' and a different vision of the world, realize that the fundamental claims of 'civilization' are both fraudulent and deceptive? What if, around the globe, a tide of rebellion is rising, expressed not through the blind rage and anger that leads to terrorism, but by an army of 'little people' who have been gifted with a radiant vision of a 'new Jerusalem'? The reaction of the establishment to such a development is likely to be one in which those who dare to preach an alternative vision of the purpose and goal of human existence will be ostracized and vilified. Their social vision will be dismissed as ridiculously impracticable, even absurd in the light of the infallible laws of the market. And there may well be a personal price to pay; throughout history those who have made the reverse journey, *from* Emmaus to Jerusalem, have appeared to pose a grave threat to the order and well-being of the city and have been lampooned as lunatics or, when their numbers reached worrying proportions, confined within gulags and labour camps where they have been taught the error of their ways, or else left to die. There is no reason to think that this pattern is about to change in a globalized world, but it just might be that the millions of little people who have 'seen the Lord' and are silently making their way back towards the city offer our fractured, endangered world the best grounds for hope that we are likely to discover today.

Back to Jerusalem

At the beginning of this book we observed the way in which the journey to Emmaus involved a retreat from the city. The urban centre, the place of terrible violence, where the claims of the Messiah have been categorically rejected, is abandoned, left behind. At the same time, the walk to Emmaus is a journey to the suburbs, to relative peace and tranquillity, where life moves at a different pace. As we noted earlier, for the despairing disciples this was a necessary retreat; these were people in urgent need of healing and recovery. However, once that healing has taken place (and taken place far more quickly than was anticipated) the disciples resolve to retrace their steps and re-enter the city. The experience they have known and the revolutionary knowledge they now possess cannot be confined within the suburbs but must be announced within the metropolitan centre. The journey from Emmaus signals something important about the relationship between a resurrection faith and an urban world and it anticipates the essentially urban character of the earliest Christian movement.

New Testament scholar Dieter Georgi has observed that most of Jesus' followers were rural people who reacted to his arrest and execution by fleeing from the city to return to the countryside in Galilee. Those who remained in Jerusalem, mainly women and a few men, joined by others who, like the Emmaus two, later returned, found themselves in an unfamiliar environment involving real danger. As Georgi puts it: 'We should not overlook the fact that remaining in or returning to Jerusalem implied the risk of extreme social insecurity.' Since almost all of Jesus' disciples appear to have been Galileans with 'the center of their lives, family, profession, and the like in Galilee', they would have had 'no background or resources in Jerusalem' (Georgi, 2005, 56). The fact that these disciples, including the apostles, now took up residence in the violent city that had rejected and murdered their Lord, signals the beginning of a revolutionary change 'entailing a new attitude to urban reality'. The source of this transformation is, as our narrative so vividly reveals, the conviction that the crucified One is alive and that witness to this world-changing truth must be made within the urban centre. Georgi suggests that these first, Jerusalem-based Easter witnesses eventually encountered visiting pilgrims from 'the Hellenistic urban culture at large', with the result that followers of Jesus travelled from Jerusalem 'into the urban culture of the Mediterranean, including the large cities such as Antioch'. There is thus a direct connection between the experience at Emmaus (together with other epiphanies within the city) and the essentially urban character of the earliest Christian movement. This urban form of the Church (discussed by Georgi in fascinating detail), set the course for Christianity for centuries to come until, with the invasion of Europe by the Germans, 'people from the backwoods took power, and Christianity turned into a rural and small-town religion and has remained so until today'. Thus, in complete contrast to the first followers of the risen Christ, Christians today find themselves living in a world that is overwhelmingly urban in character, while there is 'no real consciousness in the contemporary church of really belonging to the city as to a universal phenomenon' (2005, 67).[2]

What then are the lessons for Christians today in this 'return to Jerusalem'? Clearly, the suburbs can be places where the risen Christ, who knows no geographical or spatial limitations, can be encountered. More than that, perhaps it is sometimes absolutely necessary to exit the city in order to experience renewal and a life-transforming vision. As with the Emmaus two, retreat is not always to be viewed in a negative light, but may be the only route towards sanity and recovery. This is particularly the case when, as in the modern world, the balance between the city and nature has so often been lost and urban existence frequently involves life with minimal contact with the wonders of the created world. Mike Davis, in a disturbing book with the title *Planet of Slums*, describes the urban future that faces multiplied millions of this world's inhabitants:

> the cities of the future, rather than being made out of glass and steel as envisioned by earlier generations of urbanists, are instead largely constructed out of crude brick, straw, recycled plastic, cement blocks and scrap wood. Instead of cities of light soaring toward heaven, much of the twenty-first century urban world squats in squalor, surrounded by pollution, excrement, and decay.
>
> (Davis, 2006, 19)

In such a world there may be good and valid reasons for lodging in Emmaus. But when the epiphany comes, when vision and hope are restored and the imagination is purged of false images and renewed in line with God's priorities for the redemption of his whole creation, then it must become impossible to remain in the suburbs, sealed off from the realities of a wider urban world. Christians who have really 'seen the Lord' must retrace their steps, repent of their comfortable isolation, and build bridges which make possible a two-way traffic between the privileged and the oppressed.

Hispanic theologian and historian Justo Gonzalez observes that when the New Testament was being written, Rome viewed itself as both the greatest of all cities and the great builder of cities across the ancient world. Urbanization became a tool of imperial policy, with cities built on a Roman model dotting the landscape of the empire and submissive to the rule and ideology of the Caesars. Aelius Aristides extolled the urban achievements of Rome and boasted that 'the coasts and interiors have been filled with cities'. But, as Gonzalez points out, when John of Patmos experienced his epiphany while incarcerated in a Roman penal colony, he caught sight of another city, a new Jerusalem, beside which Rome paled into insignificance. This coming city is a place where tears and death are eliminated, where the gates never close, and peoples of every race and tribe are welcomed. Such a vision presents a radical critique of Rome, and of every city built on greed and violence, where the public image of success and well-being involves a massive cover-up that conceals from view inconvenient facts about the underside of urban life. But if this vision challenged Rome then, it also challenges complacent, suburban churches *now*:

> Just as John's vision was a challenge to Rome's vision, so it is also a challenge to our cities, cities of alabaster buildings gleaming over the homeless huddled under bridges, cities where death walks the streets at night, where children live in fear and the most common visions are the hallucinations of addicts and alcoholics. Furthermore, if John's vision is true, and a great city of love and peace is the proper image for describing God's future with humankind, what does that say about those of us who

have decided that the only way to enjoy life in peace is to abandon the city to its own misery, to create our own suburban sectarian little 'new Jerusalems' where we can live in peace while our cities burn?

(Gonzalez, 1999, 107)

The biblical narrative that has formed the text around which this book is structured leaves us with no alternative but to conclude either that suburban Christians who 'see the Lord' will be compelled to follow the Emmaus two back to the city to share their vision in the metropolitan centre, or that those same Christians, remaining in comfortable isolation and wilful ignorance of wider urban realities, *cannot have seen the Lord.*[3]

Back to the future

As the two disciples made their way along the darkened road back to the city, what kind of future might they have envisaged for the Jesus movement? In the previous discussion we have used words like 'transformed' and 'renewed' rather liberally. I do not intend now to withdraw or contradict those claims, but it may be wise to remind ourselves of the disciples' specific context so as to avoid reading back into this narrative developments that only come much later.

Once inside the city (there is no indication of how access was gained) our two walkers have some of the wind taken out of their sails by the discovery that their experience has already been paralleled within the walls of Jerusalem in an epiphany granted to Simon Peter. There is thus no need for the Emmaus two to convince those whom they previously described as 'our companions' of the authenticity of their experience, since those companions immediately bear witness to them: 'It is true! The Lord has risen and has appeared to Simon' (24.33). The story from Emmaus, which they might have anticipated would be headline news within the disciple group, thus provides supporting evidence for something already known. Christ has gone ahead of them; the knowledge of the risen One

93

cannot be reduced to the private experience of certain individuals, but is given to the disciples as a community of witness.

It is clear that at this point the apostles and a wider group of Jesus' followers took up residence within the city. What is particularly significant for this discussion is that the final sentence of Luke's Gospel points towards an answer to the question as to the kind of future the disciples now anticipated: 'And they stayed continually at the temple, praising God' (24.53). This statement reminds us that these are Jewish followers of Jesus the Messiah and although they clearly understand the momentous nature of what they have witnessed, the wider consequences of the resurrection in relation to their own faith and practice is, as yet, unknown. A mighty explosion makes an immediate and devastating impact, but the fall-out from such an event may take years, even generations, to be appreciated and understood. So here, I suggest, when our walkers made their way back towards the city they had as yet very little comprehension of what the future held.

In fact Luke, the author of both the Gospel that bears his name and the sequel, which we know as Acts of the Apostles, makes it perfectly clear that the nature of the revolution brought about by the risen Christ was at first little understood, and even when its full significance began to dawn, was stoutly resisted. Thus, when Christ appears for the final time to his disciples, we are told that they asked him whether he would now, at last, 'restore the kingdom to Israel' (Acts 1.6). Here are people who continue to think within the inherited categories of understanding and who, therefore, believe that the resurrection of Jesus could be accommodated within the existing structures of the religion. The walk back to Jerusalem might, after all, prove to be a return to the past.

After the event that we know as Pentecost, the disciples continued meeting every day in the temple courts and their pattern of worship and teaching was little different from what it had always been. They are at this point a group, a party, if you will, a *sect* within Judaism, identified by their confession of Jesus as the promised Messiah and by a radically egalitarian way of life. This community drew the admiration of fellow Jews who recognized in the Jesus movement a social model that recalled the ethical demands made upon Israel by her great prophets. The disciples presented, and they intended to present, a new social model for Israel. If the nation, drawn by their example of love and sacrificial care for each other, would turn to Jesus as Messiah, then it would become what it was always intended to be: a light to all the peoples of the earth. When that day came, the flow of Gentile proselytes would, as the prophets had predicted, become an unstoppable flood.

But none of this was to happen! As it turned out, God's future proved to be unpredictable and involved considerable discontinuity with the past. The God who had raised Jesus from the dead would be discovered at work in the world in ways that were totally unexpected and rather alarming. In one sense, this should not have been so surprising because there were precedents within Israel's history, crucial turning points at which God broke through existing concepts and traditions in ways that were completely surprising and astonishing. Thus, at one such major point of transition, a prophet is heard warning the people of Israel: 'Forget the former things; do not dwell on the past', because the 'new thing' God was to bring about would break through the bounds of all previous notions of himself and his ways of working in the world (Isaiah 43.18–19). So now, the disciples only gradually, and with considerable difficulty, come to appreciate the extent of the newness that God's future will involve, a future that will astonish and alarm the guardians of existing traditions.

The extreme difficulty of coming to terms with God's newness is indicated in the narratives to be found in the book of Acts. Luke makes it clear that the realization dawned very slowly that the changes brought about by Christ were far more revolutionary than anyone understood at the beginning. The climax of this phase is reached when the apostle Peter, after an immense personal struggle with the discovery of the universal implications of his own confession of Christ as Lord, finally throws in the towel and admits to a Gentile audience that it has taken him a very long time to recognize the shape of God's future: 'I now realise how true it is that God does not show favouritism, but accepts men from every nation who fear him and do what is right' (Acts 10.34–35).

Even then the debate is far from over; resistance to the new can be traced throughout the history of the early Christian movement and the impact of the original explosion in Jerusalem still echoes through the pages of the book of Revelation at the end of the New Testament. Justo Gonzalez suggests that when John of Patmos is told that he must 'prophesy again about many peoples, nations, languages and kings' (Revelation 10.11), a task which the author of the book indicates involved much 'bitterness', he was, in fact, being asked to challenge the ethnocentric nature of existing churches with the vision of the international, multicultural community that God intended to call into existence in the crucified and risen Christ.

> The vision which John the Jew has is of a Gentile church, a church where the Gentiles, the nations, *ta ethne*, the *goyim*, will come and take their place right next to the tribes of Israel, and all together will claim the ancient promise made to the people of Israel, that they would be a kingdom of priests. That is a vision sweet as honey, for it shows the fullness of the mercy of God; but it is also a vision bitter to the stomach, because it shows that no people, no tribe, no language, no nation, can claim a place of particular honor in that fullness. And it is bittersweet because it involves radical change in the very congregations where John has served and which he loves.
>
> (Gonzalez, 1999, 92)

The conclusion we must then reach is that when the Emmaus two made their way back towards Jerusalem, it was a journey towards a future that at that point lay beyond their powers of imagination or comprehension. They had no idea, nor could they possibly have imagined at this point, the extent of the changes that lay ahead. The idea that the temple would no longer be the focal point of worship, that divinely sanctioned rituals that had signified holiness for centuries could be set aside, and (above all) that Gentiles might enter the kingdom through faith in Christ without meeting established conditions of membership among the people of God, all of this was as yet unknown and *unknowable*. It would take decades and a long and painful struggle before the full implications of God's newness became clear.

Towards God's future

The final question that we must confront in the light of our study of this narrative now becomes clear: can we make our journey back to the future with an awareness and an acceptance of the fact that, once again, we may be facing changes far more radical than we can presently imagine and, possibly, than we actually wish to embrace? The study of the history of theology and mission in the last few years has led to an understanding of what is called 'paradigm change'. That is to say, there have been periods within that history when really radical changes have taken place as fresh insights have emerged regarding the meaning of Christ and the gospel as the outcome of the successful translation of that message into new languages and cultures. You may remember at this point the question that arose in the shadows of Glasgow Cathedral concerning the coherence of the Christian faith across the centuries in the light of its apparently kaleidoscopic varieties of expression. That variety is explained precisely by the fact that Christ enters human cultures, not as an alien, the Saviour of somebody else's world, but as the redeemer of the whole world, and of specific peoples and cultures. The Christian faith is infinitely translatable, so that the pattern shown at the beginning, in which the Gentiles became followers of Christ without the requirement that they accept the culture of those who brought the good news to them, has been repeated throughout history.

What makes our times both exciting and extremely challenging is the fact that we appear to be living through the latest and almost certainly the greatest such paradigm change in the entire history of the Christian movement. One indication of this is found in the now well-established fact of the growth of what is called 'World Christianity'. The spread of the message of Jesus across the world, and its penetration of so many different cultures is unprecedented and itself heralds significant changes in the decades ahead. Whatever else may be said about God's future in the twenty-first century, it seems certain that it will be *global* and that the normative shape of the Christian movement will cease to be determined by its previous heartlands in Europe and North America and will, instead, result from its deepening interaction with cultures across the southern hemisphere.

The challenge this presents to Western Christianity has been well expressed by Justo Gonzalez, who points out that the difficult task today is not, as many imagine, that of bringing ethnic peoples into the Christian community, but rather of accepting the global transformation in the whole shape of the Church that God has already accomplished:

> The fact is that the gospel *is* making headway among many tribes, peoples, nations, and languages – that it is indeed making more headway among them than it is among the dominant cultures of the North Atlantic. The question is not whether there will be a multicultural church. Rather, the question is whether those who have become accustomed to seeing the gospel expressed only or primarily in terms of those dominant cultures will be able to participate in the life of the multicultural church that is already a reality.
>
> (Gonzalez, 1999, 91)

For Christians in the economically, politically and militarily dominant nations of the North, who are among those who benefit most from economic globalization, it is a hard thing to come to terms with the fact that they now constitute a minority within the kingdom of God and that the dynamic centres of faith and hope are found at the peripheries of empire, predominantly among peoples who are poor and oppressed. As Gonzalez observes, rich Christians must recognize that they belong within a global community of people from all cultures who worship the Lamb, and that this implies that 'no matter what they may have thought', their own nation and language is no more in God's plan 'than *one* of the many peoples and tribes and nations and languages whom God is calling to make, as Revelation would say, "a kingdom of priests serving God"' (1999, 91–2).

The challenge of facing such a future is itself considerable. However, this aspect of the future is known and is already, to a considerable degree, a reality. I want to conclude by suggesting that on the analogy of the Emmaus experience we have explored in this book, Christians in both the North and the South may be moving towards a future that will bring other surprises which presently lie beyond our powers of prediction or imagination. This is difficult for us to accept, not least because in a culture in which it is assumed that everything is capable of measurement and analysis, it goes against the grain to suggest that what is coming towards us from the future lies outside our powers of prediction. But if the newness that God brought into being at Emmaus laid the foundation for a future that was to burst through existing categories of thought and practice, and if that pattern has been replicated again and again in Christian history, should we not prepare ourselves for the shock of the divine newness that transcends previous experience? God's future will not be extrapolated from existing trends or data, but will open up fresh horizons in the growth of his kingdom on earth. Even as these words are written, it is tempting to try to predict the shape of this newness, but wisdom and, not least, the analogy of the text we have considered here, suggest that we must simply wait in trusting confidence for the divine newness that, when it does appear, will reflect the glory of the One who raises the dead and makes all things new. In a one-dimensional world, the prospect of God's future offers our troubled age the possibility of the renewal of hope in a time of uncertainty.

Epilogue

One Sunday morning in a summer season in 1950s Paris, a visiting preacher from the United States concluded morning worship at the American Church in Quai d'Orsay and made his way towards the door to greet members of the congregation on their departure. He did so with a sense of disappointment generated by the realization that there had been a noticeable drop in the level of attendance on this morning compared with previous weeks. The explanation for this seemed obvious and rather dispiriting: on previous Sundays the organ had been played by the great musician Marcel Dupré, and this had attracted a considerable number of French people who had not now returned in the absence of such a musical attraction.

However, as the members of the congregation emerged in the porch, one man of striking appearance approached the minister with outstretched hand and said warmly: 'Monsieur, Reverend, thank you, thank you for the service.' When the minister enquired as to the stranger's name, he received an unanticipated reply: 'I am Albert Camus. I have been here four Sundays and only today did I finally get a seat.' And then, with words that eclipsed the self-pity the preacher had been tempted to feel on descending the pulpit steps, Camus added: 'For these past Sundays, I came to hear Marcel Dupré play, but today I came to hear you. Would you have lunch with me tomorrow?'

From this initial contact between the American Protestant minister, Howard Mumma, and the great French writer, Albert Camus (who we have already encountered in the first

'Dispatch from the Emmaus road' at the conclusion of Chapter 1), there developed a close friendship and a deep and fascinating dialogue that echoes many of the themes running through this book.[1] The two men did meet for lunch the next day and Camus came straight to the point, indicating that while his initial reasons for coming to church had been cultural and musical, the deeper cause was related to the fact that, as he put it, 'I am searching for something I do not have, something I'm not sure I can even define.' Thus began a remarkable friendship that extended over a number of years and resulted in conversations marked by great honesty, openness and passion. Mumma found himself drawn into a wider circle of French intellectuals, including Jean-Paul Sartre and Simone de Beauvoir, where passionate discussions took place concerning the meaning of human existence. In a manner he could never have anticipated, the Christian minister became a dialogue partner to leading French humanists in a way that beautifully fulfilled one of Camus' own most moving requests: 'Don't walk in front of me, I may not follow; don't walk behind me, I may not lead; walk beside me, and just be my friend.'

The extracts from Camus' work cited earlier in this book illustrate the exceptional integrity and clarity with which he analysed the modern condition. The themes that run through his writings – the failure of Christianity to offer an adequate theodicy in the face of the immensity of human suffering, the human longing for a meaning to life that transcends material, physical existence, and the determination to go on living for others despite the absurdity of existence in an empty, silent cosmos – all of these surfaced repeatedly during these dialogues. At one point Camus told his American friend: 'To lose one's life is a very little thing. But to lose the meaning of life, to see our reasoning disappear, is unbearable.' Mumma responded by suggesting that there were narratives within the Bible that related closely to Camus' anguished questions, and the conversational Bible studies which the two men shared together appeared to provide the writer with a renewed sense of hope. Indeed, Mumma reports that Camus astonished him with a request for Christian baptism with the words: 'I want this. This is what I want to commit my life to.'

At this point Howard Mumma made a fateful decision: uneasy about re-baptizing a French Catholic and unwilling to administer the rite of baptism in a private ceremony, he insisted that he could only meet Camus' request on condition that the writer would agree to a public ceremony linked to becoming a member of the church. Camus' request for baptism was immediately withdrawn and the writer, clearly disappointed, said firmly: 'I cannot belong to any church.' It is difficult to avoid the conclusion that the seeker's progress towards Christ had been halted by the erection of an ecclesiastical barrier that he was simply unable to cross. Shortly after this, when Mumma left Paris to return to the United States, Albert Camus went to the airport and said farewell with these words: 'My friend, *mon cheri*, thank you . . . I am going to keep striving for the Faith.' It was the last time the two men would see each other; some weeks later, back in the USA, Mumma heard the news of Albert Camus' tragic death in a road accident.

What might be the significance of this remarkable story in the context of our discussion of the walk to Emmaus in the foregoing chapters?

- First, it provides another illustration of the kind of dialogues that I have suggested need to take place in a time of multiple endings and great uncertainties. Howard Mumma was willing to befriend the French philosopher, to simply listen to him and respect his deep and profound questions.
- Second, it illustrates the grace of God at work within the world, creating the spiritual hunger and 'longing' that we have earlier noticed Kierkegaard describing. I do not wish to contradict the claim at the end of the last chapter that we must 'wait in trusting confidence' for the unveiling of God's future, but it seems certain that when this time comes it will surprise us with the discovery of just how limited has been our awareness of the extent of Christ's grace at work in the world.

- Third, it poses difficult questions concerning the form of the Church in the future. In later life Howard Mumma agonized over his response to Camus' request for baptism and wondered whether he had made a great mistake. Had Camus not, in reality, been far closer to Christ than many church members who belonged to the institution but were complete strangers to the kind of spiritual and intellectual struggle of honest seekers? If, as I believe, this experience provides a hint of the shape of God's surprising future in the century ahead, how might we reimagine and reshape the Christian community so that it ceases to be an obstacle to those who seek for truth? What kind of Church might be able to nurture discipleship within its bounds, while remaining open and welcoming to the evidence of epiphanies within other communities where people who had lost hope and cried to heaven for help have found an unknown Stranger draw near and set their hearts ablaze?

These, I suspect, are some of the questions we will have to face in the light of God's new future in the coming century.

We treasure what you end:
A prayer by Walter Brueggemann[2]

We confess that we are set today in the midst
  of your awesome, awful work.
We will, because we have no alternative,
  be present this day
  to your dreadful work of termination.
We will watch while you pull down
  and dismantle
  that with which you are finished.
We will, because we have no alternative,
  be present today
  to your dream-filled work
  of evoking,
  imagining,
  forming,
  and inviting.
We are double-minded in your presence,
  because we treasure what you end
  and we fear what you conjure –
  but we are your people
  and trust you all this day
  in your awesome,
  awful work.
Override our reluctance
  and take us with you
  in justice
  and mercy
  and peace.
Take us with you in your overriding,
  that our day may be a day of joy
  and well-being
  and newness
  from your very hand.
In the name of your decisive newness,
  even Jesus. Amen.

Loyola University, Bastille Day, 14 July 1989

Notes and acknowledgements

1 The despairing journey

1 The phrase quoted here concerning Caravaggio's work comes from Simon Schama's great book *Rembrandt's Eyes* (1999), p. 250. See also W. A. Visser 't Hooft, *Rembrandt and the Gospel* (1957) and Jane Dillenberger, *Style and Content in Christian Art* (1965), especially pp. 181–99.

2 I have not attempted to analyse the crisis facing modern civilization. Kowlakowski's book *Modernity on Endless Trial* (1990) is an important study of this subject. On the religious crisis see Steve Bruce, *God is Dead: Secularization in the West* (2002). One of the most original and disturbing studies related to this theme is Zygmunt Bauman's *Modernity and the Holocaust* (2000). Bauman argues that the terrible events of the Holocaust, often interpreted as a *departure* from the values of civilized society, actually occurred 'at a high stage of our civilization and at the peak of human cultural achievement, and for this reason it is a problem for that society, civilization and culture' (2000, x). His detailed study leads him to conclude that the Holocaust was 'a rare, yet significant and reliable, test of the hidden possibilities of modern society' (2000, 12). Perhaps more than any other book published in recent times, this volume places a large question mark against many of the Enlightenment's most basic assumptions. At a different level Christopher Lasch's book *The Culture of Narcissism: American Life in an Age of Diminishing Expectations* (1979) charts the decline of vision and hope and the impact of this on individuals within the United States. 'Today Americans are overcome not by the sense of endless possibility but by the banality of the social order they have erected against it. Having internalized the social restraints by means of which they formerly sought to keep possibility within civilized limits, they feel themselves overwhelmed by annihilating boredom, like animals whose instincts have withered in captivity' (1979, 11). Finally, a brief but important study by Michael Ignatieff parallels the work of Jeremy Seabrook cited within this chapter. See his *The Needs of Strangers* (1994).

3 Colin Chapman's book *Islam and the West* (1998), from which this quotation is taken, is a valuable study of this subject from a Christian perspective. For a fascinating examination of the same theme from a Muslim angle, see Akbar Ahmed, *Postmodernism and Islam: Predicament*

and Promise (1992). After I had begun writing this book I discovered a volume edited by J. Dudley Woodberry bearing the title *Muslims and Christians on the Emmaus Road* (1989). In the introduction the editor observes that today countless Muslims *literally* walk along the Emmaus road. 'And hundreds of years after Cleopas and his friend had their discussion on the way to Emmaus, Muslims echo their conversation about the man who died on a cross.'

4 Reproduced by permission of Penguin Books Ltd.
5 Reproduced by permission of Penguin Books Ltd.

2 Christians on the Emmaus road

1 The last time I drove past this church its plea to the world had evidently been answered; it was surrounded by scaffolding and the previous banner had been replaced by an advertisement for Renault cars covering the entire length of the building. Yet again, there is a strange irony here: Renault advertised a new model some time back with the phrases 'The Power' over the engine and 'The Glory' over the interior. Perhaps it is not surprising that the 'Creator of Automobiles' should come to the rescue of the church, but the affair reveals the depths of Christianity's captivity to the culture of economism and its tragic ignorance of the ways in which its own sacred language is first purloined, and then harnessed to the goals of consumerism.

2 See Edward Said, *Orientalism* (1995). On the relevance of Said's work to Christian missions, see Herb Swanson, 'Said's *Orientalism* and the Study of Christian Missions' (Swanson, 2004).

3 The poem is taken from *Dennis O'Driscoll: New and Selected Poems* published by Anvil Press Poetry in 2004.

4 Reprinted by permission of Eerdmans. This volume is still in print and may be purchased at www.eerdmans.com.

5 Reproduced by kind permission of Continuum International Publishing Group.

3 The unknown Christ

1 The sociologist of religion, David Martin, has observed that the foundational vision of Christianity is rooted in 'the kingship of the lowly king, and in the eschatological anticipation of a time when "the kingdoms of this world shall become the kingdoms of our God and of his Christ"'. In the New Testament, he notes, the attributes of glory are 'transferred to the "sacred diadem" which on Calvary's hill was nothing but a crown of thorns'. It is this paradox, Martin says, that 'lies at the heart of Christian civilization and its discontents'; especially the 'oscillations between the power and glory of the Church established on earth as the bearer of the keys of the kingdom, and the power and glory

that belongs to a man expelled from the city as a blasphemer and a criminal'. Martin goes on to draw a contrast between the foundational vision of the Christian faith and that of Islam which originates 'in a prophet who succeeds as a conqueror and is part of a lineage'. Consequently, Islam finds no problem in understanding the 'secular' in terms of power and lineage, but it does not 'generate radical peace movements or monastic fraternities or sororities'. See David Martin, *On Secularization: Towards a Revised General Theory* (2005), pp. 172–3.

2 I have discussed the ambiguous nature of the historical inheritance of Christianity in Europe in *Mission After Christendom* (2003). What may be called the 'European phase' of Christian history provides tragic examples of the kinds of compromises being discussed here, from the alliance of missionaries with *conquistadores* to the interconnected nature of Protestant missions and colonial expansion in the modern period. It seems to me particularly important to listen to the prophetic voices of people from these periods who understood the ways in which the name of Christ was being dishonoured and misrepresented and called their contemporaries to repentance and discipleship. I have attempted to recover and give voice to two such forgotten prophets in 'The Forgotten "Grandfather" of Protestant Mission? Perspectives on Globalization from Jean de Léry' (Smith, 2006); and 'A Victorian Prophet Without Honour: Edward Miall and the Critique of Nineteenth-Century British Christianity' in Stephen Clark (ed.), *Tales of Two Cities: Christianity and Politics* (Smith, 2005), pp. 152–83. That this is not, however, simply a historical issue is evident when one considers the manner in which the Bible is used at the present time to justify the imperialist policies of the current government in the USA. A disturbing example of this can be found in Michael D. Evans' best-selling book, *The American Prophecies: Ancient Scriptures Reveal Our Nation's Future* (2004). This author interprets the Bible in a manner that provides sanction for American foreign policy, including the invasion of Iraq and a predicted war against Syria, and discovers indications of divine blessing upon the United States in the fact that the nation possesses 'more than half the world's wealth' while comprising only 7 per cent of its population. This latest and somewhat bizarre example of what Martin Luther called a 'theology of glory' serves to underline the truth of the conclusion of Douglas John Hall: 'Whatever survives into the future of the Christian faith will have to achieve greater depths of wisdom and courage than most of what has transpired . . . throughout 1500 years of Christendom' (Hall, 2003, 10).

4 Epiphany!

1 Samuel Barber was deeply influenced by Kierkegaard's works which became widely known in the United States in the 1930s. Barber described the Danish

philosopher as 'a major literary figure and an exciting but enigmatic intellectual force'. His beautiful settings of Kierkegaard's prayers have been recorded by the Chicago Symphony Orchestra and Chorus, conducted by Andrew Schenck (Koch International Classics, 3-7125-2H1, 1991).

2 Madeleine Bunting suggests that if the secular left is to be 'coaxed into a more knowledgeable and intelligent conversation on religion, then those of faith have a comparably large mountain to climb'. People with religious faith will have to recognize two non-negotiables in the discussion: 'First, the secularism of political life . . . has sunk deep and precious roots for good reasons and that should not be reversed – no jockeying for institutional advantage please. Second, no exclusive claims for any tradition. Instead what's needed is an ever-ready openness to understand the metaphors of other faiths' (Bunting, 2006).

3 I use the word 'holy' here in the sense that it has been defined by Rudolf Otto in his influential book *Das Heilige* (1917). Otto observed that the term 'holy' is usually understood as an ethical category, but he argued that this is in fact its secondary, derivative sense and that its original point of reference related to what he called the experience of the *numinous*. 'It is the emotion of a creature, submerged and overwhelmed by its own nothingness in contrast to that which is supreme above all creatures' (Otto, 1958, 10). It is precisely such a religious experience that is described in the story of the Emmaus walk and Rembrandt's depiction of the moment of recognition captures this experience in a way that, as far as I am aware, is unique in Western art.

4 An example can be found in the work of one of the twentieth century's most perceptive social and cultural analysts, Ernest Becker: 'In our time we have seen the *demonic* emerge in all its starkness . . . [it] comes into being for man whenever he is manipulated by large, impersonal forces beyond his control, forces that he is actively and uncritically contributing to' (Becker, 1968, 141).

5 The quotation comes from the prologue to Jack Miles' book *Christ: A Crisis in the Life of God*. The prologue bears the title 'Crucifixion and the Conscience of the West' and Miles makes this observation: 'Winners usually look like winners, and losers look like losers. But thanks to this paradoxical feature of the Christian myth, there remains lodged deep in the political consciousness of the West a readiness to believe that the apparent loser may be the real winner unrecognized. In Christianity's epilogue to the God-story that it inherited from Judaism, the Lord God becomes human without ceasing to be the Lord and, unrecognized by all but a few, experiences the human condition at its worst before winning in the end a glorious victory' (Miles, 2001, 3–4).

6 Like Becker before him, Zygmunt Bauman has examined the subject of the human dread of death, and the impact of this on the shape of human

cultures, in considerable detail. In 1992 he published *Mortality, Immortality and Other Life Strategies* in which he suggests that the necessity of living constantly with the awareness of human mortality provides a key to the understanding of 'many a crucial aspect of social and cultural organization of all known societies'. More recently Bauman has returned to this subject again in the book *Liquid Fear* (2006), in which he repeats his belief that all human cultures must be understood as being 'ingenious contraptions calculated to make life with the awareness of mortality liveable' (2006, 31). However, under the conditions created by what Bauman has called 'liquid modernity', it becomes more difficult than ever to confront death since, as he puts it: 'looking death in its bare face is all but unbearable'. He adds this perceptive comment: 'This is why manipulation can bring huge profits, and contains few if any risks: it can count on a grateful clientele among the millions trying desperately to avert their eyes from Gorgon's face' (2006, 51).

7 Becker, whose words are quoted here, published a series of remarkable books dealing with the subjects of evil and death, including *The Structure of Evil* (1968), *The Denial of Death* (1973), and his final work, completed just before his own death, *Escape From Evil* (1975). He argued convincingly that the human urge to deny mortality was the root cause of evil. His comments on Christianity remain challenging: the Christian story retains its redemptive power but this is undermined by the fact that the religion has failed 'to offer its ideal of heroic sainthood as an immediate personal one to be lived by all believers'. The promise of the early Church to bring about social justice has never been realized and modern Christianity seems as far from this hope as ever: 'the churches still bless unheroic wars and sanctify group hatred and victimage' (Becker, 1975, 163–4). At the end of his profound study of evil in human society Becker makes this statement: '*If* we were not fear-stricken animals who repressed awareness of ourselves and our world, *then* we would live in peace and unafraid of death, trusting to our Creator God and celebrating His creation' (Becker, 1975, 164).

5 Return to the city

1 My admiration for Zygmunt Bauman's work will, I hope, be obvious from the use I have made of it elsewhere in this book. I regard him as the most important analyst of contemporary culture at work today and I believe his ground-breaking book *Modernity and the Holocaust* to be one of the most remarkable and important works to have appeared in the last fifty years. Bauman's discussions of human mortality and the huge impact that the fear of death has upon human life and culture are full of insight and challenge. In *Liquid Fear* (2006) he describes

the present state of the world in unremittingly dark colours, yet argues that it is the task of intellectuals to keep hope alive. Very occasionally Bauman hints at the possibility of a source of meaning that transcends the material world (as when he argues that we must 'trust' that values are 'eternal' and truths are 'universal'). However, Bauman's analysis operates within a materialist framework that leaves him ultimately struggling to discover a secure foundation for hope. Thus, the final chapter of *Liquid Fear* is entitled 'Thought Against Fear (or, an inconclusive conclusion for those who may ask what might be done)'. I am suggesting above that the Christian belief in the resurrection of Christ provides a solid foundation for hope and that, without for one moment downplaying the desperate seriousness of the human plight, it also provides the dynamic for living life 'against the grain' of the spirit of our times.

2 Dieter Georgi's *The City in the Valley: Biblical Interpretation and Urban Theology* (2005) is full of fresh insights with regard to the urban character of early Christianity. However, I part company with him at a number of points, in particular his assertion that Jesus 'sanctified Galilee by his origin and presence' and that when his disciples chose to take up residence within the city of Jerusalem, they did so 'despite their Galilean origin and their experience with Jesus in that region' (2005, 56). It is true, of course, that the teaching of Jesus reflects a rural context, but I think Georgi overlooks the extent to which, then as now, urbanization involved not merely the expansion of the population of cities, but the spread of urban culture and values throughout society. As Horsley and Silberman note, 'at the time of Jesus, a growing bureaucracy closely connected to the court of Antipas played a crucial role in creating a crisis of debt and dispossession that touched and transformed the lives of nearly every family in Galilee' (Horsley and Silberman, 1997, 26). Galilee was no isolated, rural backwater, immune from the impact of an increasingly urban world. What is more, the impact of rural poverty on the young, with men being attracted to the urban centres of the ancient world to seek employment and freedom from traditional values is clearly reflected in the familiar parable of the Prodigal Son in Luke 15.11–31.

3 On the challenges facing suburban Christianity, see Albert Hsu, *The Suburban Christian: Finding Spiritual Vitality in the Land of Plenty* (2006).

Epilogue

1 These conversations are described in Howard Mumma's *Albert Camus and the Minister* (2000). The author published them in his ninetieth year, long after the events had taken place. He acknowledged that since his

conversations with Camus were of a private and intimate nature, it was impossible to guarantee the strict accuracy of his recollection of what was said on each occasion. However, he had made private notes following these meetings and there seems to be no reason to question the authenticity and accuracy of the general picture that emerges from this remarkable document.

2 This beautiful prayer, which makes such a fitting conclusion to the present study, comes from a volume containing the prayers which Walter Brueggemann used before lecturing on the Old Testament. See 'We treasure what you end', from Walter Brueggemann, *Awed to Heaven, Rooted in Earth: Prayers of Walter Brueggemann*, ed. Edwin Searcy (2002), p. 27.

Bibliography

Ahmed, Akbar, 1992, *Postmodernism and Islam: Predicament and Promise* (London: Routledge)

Alison, James, 2005, 'Resurrection Hope and the Intelligence of the Victim', in Simon Barrow and Jonathan Bartley (eds), *Consuming Passion: Why the Killing of Jesus Really Matters* (London: Darton, Longman & Todd)

Bauckham, Richard, 1993, *The Theology of the Book of Revelation* (Cambridge: Cambridge University Press)

Bauman, Zygmunt, 1992, *Mortality, Immortality and Other Life Strategies* (Cambridge: Polity Press)

Bauman, Zygmunt, 2000, *Modernity and the Holocaust* (Cambridge: Polity Press)

Bauman, Zygmunt, 2006, *Liquid Fear* (Cambridge: Polity Press)

Becker, Ernest, 1968, *The Structure of Evil: An Essay on the Unification of the Science of Man* (New York: The Free Press)

Becker, Ernest, 1973, *The Denial of Death* (New York: The Free Press)

Becker, Ernest, 1975, *Escape From Evil* (New York: The Free Press)

Berger, Peter, 1961, *The Noise of Solemn Assemblies* (New York: Doubleday)

Black, Edith, 1973, 'A Rediscovery of the Christian Faith', *Radical Religion*, Volume 1, Winter: 18–20

Bosch, David, 1975, *Theology of Mission*, Course notes for 'Missiology and the Science of Religion', Pretoria: University of South Africa

Brierley, Peter, 2000, *The Tide is Running Out* (London: Christian Research)

Bruce, Steve, 2002, *God is Dead: Secularization in the West* (Oxford: Blackwell Publishers)

Brueggemann, Walter, 2000, *Texts that Linger, Words that Explode: Listening to Prophetic Voices* (Minneapolis: Fortress Press)

Bunting, Madeleine, 2006, 'Faith can make a vital contribution to both democracy and scientific ethics', *Guardian*, 19 June

Camus, Albert, 1961, *Resistance, Rebellion and Death* (London: Hamish Hamilton)

Camus, Albert, 1971, *The Rebel* (Harmondsworth: Penguin)

Camus, Albert, 1975, *The Myth of Sisyphus* (Harmondsworth: Penguin)

Chapman, Colin, 1998, *Islam and the West* (Carlisle: Paternoster Press)

Clements, Keith, 1999, *Faith on the Frontier: A Life of J. H. Oldham* (Edinburgh: T & T Clark)

Cragg, Kenneth, 1978, *Islam and the Muslim* (Milton Keynes: Open University Press)

Cragg, Kenneth, 1998, *The Secular Experience of God* (Leominster: Gracewing)

Bibliography

Davis, Mike, 2006, *Planet of Slums* (London: Verso Press)

Dillenberger, Jane, 1965, *Style and Content in Christian Art* (London: SCM Press)

Ellul, Jacques, 1973, *Hope in Time of Abandonment* (Grand Rapids: Eerdmans)

Ellul, Jacques, 1975, *The New Demons* (London: Mowbrays)

Ellul, Jacques, 1986, *The Subversion of Christianity* (Grand Rapids: Eerdmans)

Evans, Michael D., 2004, *The American Prophecies: Ancient Scriptures Reveal Our Nation's Future* (New York: Warner Faith)

Garaudy, Roger, 1976, *The Alternative Future: A Vision of Christian Marxism* (Harmondsworth: Penguin)

Georgi, Dieter, 2005, *The City in the Valley: Biblical Interpretation and Urban Theology* (Atlanta: Society of Biblical Literature)

Gonzalez, Justo L., 1999, *For the Healing of the Nations: The Book of Revelation in an Age of Cultural Conflict* (New York: Orbis Books)

Goricheva, Tatiana, 1986, *Talking about God is Dangerous: My Experiences in the East and in the West* (London: SCM Press)

Hall, Douglas John, 2003, *The Cross in our Context: Jesus and the Suffering World* (Minneapolis: Fortress Press).

Hollindale, R. J. (ed.), 1977, *A Nietzsche Reader* (Harmondsworth: Penguin)

Horsley, Richard A. and Silberman, Neil Asher, 1997, *The Message of the Kingdom: How Jesus and Paul Ignited a Revolution and Transformed the Ancient World* (Minneapolis: Fortress Press)

Hsu, Albert, 2006, *The Suburban Christian: Finding Spiritual Vitality in the Land of Plenty* (Downers Grove: InterVarsity Press)

Ignatieff, Michael, 1994, *The Needs of Strangers* (London: Vintage Books)

John Paul II, 2003, *Ecclesia in Europa* (London: Catholic Truth Society)

Kowlakowski, Leszek, 1990, *Modernity on Endless Trial* (Chicago: University of Chicago Press)

Lasch, Christopher, 1979, *The Culture of Narcissism: American Life in an Age of Diminishing Expectations* (New York: W. W. Norton)

Lochman, Jan Milic, 1988, *Christ and Prometheus? A Quest for Theological Identity* (Geneva: World Council of Churches)

Martin, David, 2005, *On Secularization: Towards a Revised General Theory* (Aldershot: Ashgate)

Metz, Johann Baptist, 1981, *The Emergent Church* (New York: Crossroad)

Miles, Jack, 2001, *Christ: A Crisis in the Life of God* (London: William Heinemann)

Moltmann, Jürgen, 1974, *The Crucified God* (London: SCM Press)

Mumma, Howard, 2000, *Albert Camus and the Minister* (Brewster, MA: Paraclete Press)

Murray, Stuart, 2004, *Post-Christendom: Church and Mission in a Strange New World* (Carlisle: Paternoster Press)

Niebuhr, H. Richard, 1929, *The Social Sources of Denominationalism* (Cleveland: Meridian Books)

Bibliography

O'Driscoll, Dennis, 2004, *Dennis O'Driscoll: New and Selected Poems* (London: Anvil Press Poetry)

Otto, Rudolf, 1958, *The Idea of the Holy: An Inquiry into the Non-rational Factor in the Idea of the Divine and its Relation to the Rational* (Oxford: Oxford University Press)

Padwick, Constance, 1961, *Muslim Devotions: A Study of Prayer Manuals in Common Use* (London: SPCK)

Pelikan, Jaroslav, 1985, *Jesus Through the Centuries: His Place in the History of Culture* (New York: Harper & Row)

Pullman, Philip, 2004, 'The Art of Reading in Colour', *Index on Censorship*, 33/4, October: 156–63

Ramachandra, Vinoth, 2003, 'Iraq, the West and the Church's Mission', *Global Connections Newsletter*, May: 4–6

Russell, Jenni, 2005, 'Even humanists feel the joy of a proper religious festival', *Guardian*, 24 December: 24

Said, Edward, 1995, *Orientalism* (London: Penguin)

Schama, Simon, 1999, *Rembrandt's Eyes* (London: Penguin)

Seabrook, Jeremy, 2003, *A World Growing Old* (London: Pluto Press)

Searcy, Edwin (ed.), 2002, *Awed to Heaven, Rooted to Earth: Prayers of Walter Brueggemann* (Minnesota: Augsburg Fortress)

Smith, David, 2003, *Mission After Christendom* (London: Darton, Longman & Todd)

Smith, David, 2005, 'A Victorian Prophet Without Honour: Edward Miall and the Critique of Nineteenth-century British Christianity', in Stephen Clark (ed.), *Tales of Two Cities: Christianity and Politics* (Leicester: InterVarsity Press): 152–83

Smith, David, 2006, 'The Forgotten "Grandfather" of Protestant Mission?: Perspectives on Globalization from Jean de Lery', *Missiology*, XXXIV/3, July: 349–59

Stendahl, Krister, 1976, *Paul Among Jews and Gentiles* (Philadelphia: Fortress Press)

Swanson, Herb, 2004, 'Said's *Orientalism* and the Study of Christian Missions', *International Bulletin of Missionary Research*, 28/3, July: 107–12

Thielicke, Helmut, 1965, *The Trouble with the Church: A Call for Renewal* (London: Hodder & Stoughton)

Tillich, Paul, 1962, *The Shaking of the Foundations* (Harmondsworth: Penguin)

Vahanian, Gabriel, 1957, *The Death of God: The Culture of our Post-Christian Era* (New York: George Braziller)

Visser 't Hooft, W. A., 1957, *Rembrandt and the Gospel* (London: SCM Press)

Walsh, Brian J. and Keesmaat, Sylvia C., 2004, *Colossians Remixed: Subverting the Empire* (Downers Grove: InterVarsity Press)

Woodberry, J. Dudley (ed.), 1989, *Muslims and Christians on the Emmaus Road* (Monrovia, CA: MARC Publications)

Index of biblical references

Index of subjects

Index of subjects